TIGER
TRAITS

TIGER
TRAITS

9 SUCCESS SECRETS you can
discover from TIGER WOODS
to be a BUSINESS CHAMPION

NATE BOOTH

HARRISON ACORN PRESS, LLC
LAS VEGAS

This book and the author are not
affiliated with or endorsed by Tiger Woods.

Quotes on pages 39, 42, 43, 44, 51, and 130 from *In Search of Tiger: A Journey Through Golf with Tiger Woods* by Tom Callahan, © 2003 by Tom Callahan. Used by permission of Crown Publishers.

Material on the Hero's Journey from The Writer's Journey: Mythic Structure for Writers by Christopher Vogler, © 1998 by Christopher Vogler. Used by permission of Michael Weiss Productions, publishers.

Distributed by Harrison Acorn Press

For ordering information or special discounts for bulk purchases, please contact Harrison Acorn Press at 1930 Village Center Circle, Ste. 3-747, Las Vegas, NV 89134, 702-444-1362.

Publisher's Cataloging-In-Publication Data
Booth, Nate.
    Tiger traits : 9 success secrets you can discover from Tiger Woods to be a business champion / Nate Booth. -- 1st ed.

        p. ; cm.

    Includes bibliographical references and index.
    ISBN-13: 978-0-9649500-3-0
    ISBN-10: 0-9649500-3-0

1. Success in business.   2. Self-actualization (Psychology)   3. Woods, Tiger--Psychology. I. Title.

HF5386 .B66 2007
650.1   2006938253

ISBN 10: 0-9649500-3-0
ISBN 13: 978-0-9649500-3-0

Printed in the United States of America on acid-free paper

07 08 09 10 11 12   10 9 8 7 6 5 4 3 2 1

First Edition

*To Mom's side of family, who provided
the writing genes that made this book possible:*

*Grandpa Jack Harrison—the editor of the small-town
newspaper, The Oakland, Iowa Acorn.*

*My Uncle John Harrison—the author of three nonfiction
books and a journalism professor at the University of
Iowa and Penn State University.*

*And Mary Lou Harrison Booth—a loving mom
who taught all us kids to be creative, giving,
and entertaining.*

TIGER
TRAITS

CONTENTS

ACKNOWLEDGMENTS

ONLY ONE AUTHOR'S NAME appears on the cover of this book, but there are dozens of people who have contributed to its quality. I would like to thank these people. First of all, I would like to thank my wife, Linda, who has tolerated my many hours at the computer writing *Tiger Traits*.

Thanks to all the people who took the time to read the manuscript and give me valuable suggestions. The PGA Head Golf Professional at TPC Summerlin, Lee Smith, examined the manuscript from a golf pro's point of view.

As editors, the talented Vicki St. George and Karen Risch at Just Write wordsmithed my manuscript into a book that I believe you'll find enjoyable to read and valuable to use. I think you will agree that Greenleaf Book Group created a striking cover design and book layout that will energize your use of the book.

Finally, I would like to thank Tiger Woods for being such an inspiring role model for millions of people around the world, and his parents, Earl and Tida, for effectively and lovingly raising a prodigy who is making the world a better place on and off the golf course.

YOUR PRE-GAME WARM-UP

SOMETIMES, GENIUS SHOWS UP EARLY. When Tiger Woods was ten months old, he was watching his dad, Earl, hit golf balls from a mat into a net Earl had set up in the garage. Tiger climbed down from his high chair, grabbed a small club his dad had made for him, placed a ball on the mat, looked at the target, and then executed an exact mirror image of Earl's swing, smacking the ball perfectly into the net. "I was flabbergasted!" Earl said later. "I almost fell off my chair. It was the most frightening thing I had ever seen!"

At first, Tiger hit the ball like left-handers do. After all, he watched his dad swing right-handed and simply executed a perfect mirror-image copy of it. Two weeks after his dramatic first shot, his dad put him on the other side of the ball. Tiger immediately reversed his grip on the club and, without missing a beat, smacked the ball perfectly from the right-handed position.

From the auspicious beginning in his dad's garage at the age of ten months, Tiger Woods is well on his way to becoming the greatest golfer of all time. Through the PGA Championship in 2006, Tiger has won fifty-four Professional Golf Association (PGA)

Tour events. He is the youngest player to win all four major professional tournaments*, and the only golfer ever to be the reigning champion in all four major tournaments at the same time. In 2006, it's estimated that he earned almost $100 million in prize money, appearance fees, and product endorsements.

More important than all his golf accomplishments, however, is the kind of person and role model he has become. Tiger is both a superlative professional golfer and an extremely successful businessperson. Since he was twenty years old he has been the head of a multimillion-dollar sports empire. Tiger signed his first deal with Nike for $50 million right after his third U.S. Amateur victory—before he won his first professional tournament, the Las Vegas Open at the TPC Summerlin course. (It's interesting that as I write, I'm overlooking the ninth hole at TPC Summerlin.) The Tiger Woods Foundation he established in 1996 helps thousands of children to reach their highest potential. Today Tiger is well on his way to being recognized both as the greatest golfer of all time, the first sports billionaire, and an exceptional philanthropist—all at the age of thirty-one!

The Nine Tiger Trait Lessons

Tiger's success in golf—and in life—is not an accident. There's no doubt that he was born with a special talent when it comes to golf, but he also possesses nine traits that have allowed him to express that talent in record-setting ways. *The American Heritage Dictionary* defines a trait as "a characteristic, especially one that distinguishes an individual from another."

---

*There are four major championships played each year—the Masters Tournament, the U.S. Open, the British Open, and the PGA Championship. Collectively, they are called the majors.

I believe that you can study a person's traits and learn valuable lessons from each one. In the same way these nine traits have made Tiger a champion, the lessons they teach will provide you with a solid foundation for an outstanding business career and a fulfilling life.

The number nine has a special significance in the golfing world. I learned to play golf on a nine-hole course in the small town of Harlan, Iowa. Most golf courses have eighteen holes divided into two sets of nine—the front (first) nine and the back (last) nine. Golf courses are sometimes called golf links because the holes are geographically linked together. (You finish one hole and walk directly to the next tee to play another hole.) The nine lessons you will learn in this book are also linked: you must learn each lesson in order to move on the next one.

Each hole, or chapter, focuses on one Tiger Trait. By "playing" each hole—reading the chapter and then putting the trait to work—you, too, can become a champion in the sport of life.

Here are the nine traits you'll be studying—the "holes" you will be playing.

Tiger Trait #1: Identify and develop natural talents.

Tiger Trait #2: Create a clear and compelling dream.

Tiger Trait #3: Select teachers, heroes, and teammates who guide, inspire, and support.

Tiger Trait #4: Be confident.

Tiger Trait #5: Manufacture magnificent mental models.

Tiger Trait #6: Let actions do the talking.

Tiger Trait #7: Constantly improve in good times and bad.

Tiger Trait #8: Be likeable.

Tiger Trait #9: Be grateful, give back.

The Power of Modeling

For ten years, I had the interesting and rewarding experience of working with Anthony Robbins in the creation and delivery of corporate training programs. Tony is recognized all over the world as an expert on peak performance and motivation, and he taught me two vital lessons: (1) Success is not an accident, and (2) success leaves clues.

Tony showed me how to effectively model others to increase the speed and odds of achieving any goal. When you practice modeling, you find someone who has done what you would like to do. You pick their brains and observe them in action if possible. You discover how they think and what they do. Then you think and act in similar ways. It's that simple.

There are two ways you can learn life's lessons: from the school of hard knocks, or from other people's experiences. The first way can be effective, but it's slow, expensive, and arduous. The second way is highly effective, fast, and fun. Successful corporations know about modeling. When they model internally, they call it best practices. When they model other companies, they call it benchmarking.

> *People never improve unless they look to some standard or example higher and better than themselves.*
> —Tryon Edwards

When you model, you take a rich person to lunch. When I say rich, I don't necessarily mean financially rich; I mean someone who has achieved what you'd like to do. And when I say take them to lunch, I don't mean that you actually take them to a restaurant. I mean you learn from them in person or by reading about them.

It's vital that you choose the right people to model. I'm amused when I see friends who want to improve their marriages and then they seek advice from people who've been divorced four times. Not a good choice—those people are good at divorce, not successful marriage! My friends should talk to couples that have been married for dozens of years and still have the energy, love, and passion flowing.

I believe Tiger Woods is an excellent model for any business-person. The nine lessons exemplified by his life and career are lessons that you and every member of your business team must learn. A few of the lessons are ones you may have expected; a few of them may surprise you. Either way, their value is proven by the life of a man who is wise and successful beyond his years.

Preview of Tiger Trait #1

When Tiger hopped out of his chair at the age of ten months and performed the perfect golf swing from both sides of the ball, it was the first signal that he was a "Mozart" in the making. I believe that the study of geniuses is intriguing because there is one lurking in each of us. The next chapter will show you how to discover and develop your inner genius.

TIGER TRAIT# ①

IDENTIFY AND DEVELOP
NATURAL TALENTS

IN THE PRE-GAME WARM-UP, you learned about Tiger's electrifying exploits in his dad's garage at the age of ten months. Even before that eye-popping occasion, Earl and his wife, Tida (pronounced Teeda), witnessed incidents that foreshadowed Tiger's budding natural talents. When Tida was pregnant with Tiger, Earl played in a golf tournament in northern California. Tida walked with Earl while he played, and as they walked the course Tiger was very active—until they reached the greens. Whenever Earl would get ready to putt, Tiger would be very quiet. It was as if he knew golf etiquette while still in the womb. Then, when Tiger was just a baby, Earl would take him into the garage while he practiced his swing, hitting golf balls into a net. For upwards of two hours, Tiger would watch Earl without making a sound. The six-month-old baby seemed already fascinated with the game.

As a toddler, Tiger ignored the toys most kids his age would choose. He preferred hitting a tennis ball "golf style" with a vacuum hose around the house for hours on end. When he was eighteen months old, his dad let him to play one hole on his first real golf course. Tiger proceeded to shoot an eleven on a 410-yard par-four hole. At the age of two, Tiger entered a tournament for boys ages ten and under—and won. When he was three, he broke fifty for the first time by shooting a forty-eight for nine holes. He had his first hole in one at the age of six—two of them, in fact!

Tiger didn't just excel in the physical aspects of the game; he always thought like a golfer. His father, Earl, reported that before his son knew how to add, the little boy know the difference between a par-four hole and par-five hole. He knew what a birdie, par, bogey, and double-bogey were, and he would keep track of the scores of his dad and other golfers as he walked with them around the course.

At an early age, Tiger wasn't just successful on the local level. Before the age of eighteen, Tiger had won six Optimist International Junior World titles. Between the ages of fifteen and seventeen, he won three consecutive U.S. Junior Amateur Championships—the first person to accomplish that feat.

Talents and Weaknesses

I don't believe he's a god,
but I believe he was sent by one.
—Michael Jordan

I think Tiger would agree with his friend Michael's statement, and quickly add, "We all were sent by one." I believe we're all born with a unique set of talents and weaknesses. Our talents are the activities where we naturally shine, and our weaknesses are the activities where we have challenges. It's easy to see that Tiger Woods' talent is playing golf. That talent was identified at a very early age and developed with years of training and practice. This has allowed Tiger to develop his talent to its full extent. If the talent hadn't been identified or developed, you very probably never would have heard of Tiger Woods.

> *As tools become rusty, so does the mind;*
> *a garden uncared for soon becomes smothered in weeds;*
> *a talent neglected withers and dies.*
>   —Ethel Page

When it comes to success, identifying and managing your weakness is just as important as identifying and developing your talents. As a hypothetical example, let's say a weakness for Tiger is fixing things around the house. He could receive all the training in the world, but he still would never become a handyman. However, Tiger could manage his weakness by having others do any home improvement projects for him.

The study of talents and weaknesses is interesting to me because for many years I ignored my own. As a kid, I always excelled in written and oral communication. I loved writing stories in school. I talked with my fifth grade teacher, Miss Schrader, a couple of years ago, and she still remembers some of my creative efforts fifty years later. I gave an original, humorous speech at high school speech contests and always received the highest rating. But for all the wrong reasons (money and prestige), I decided to become a dentist. Dentistry didn't play to my talents; I had the worst manual dexterity in my class. I should have realized this fact two years into dental school and dropped out to study writing or communication. But I felt I had to stick with my original, ill-conceived decision instead.

I practiced dentistry for ten years and was miserable the whole time. I tried to improve my skills and enjoyment level, but that's very hard to do if manual dexterity is your weakness. At forty-five years of age, I finally figured out the best use of my natural talents: I decided to speak and write about how to be successful in life. I love it. Today I'm soaring with my talents. I spend most of my time speaking and writing and learning how to improve those two skills. I also manage my weaknesses: I stay clear of glass objects and anything that requires improving or fixing around the house. Instead, I hire someone else to do it.

Three Myths About Talents and Weaknesses

In their entertaining and educational book, *Soar With Your Strengths*, Donald Clifton and Paula Nelson discuss the myths associated with talents and weaknesses. Here, in modified form, are three of them.

> **Myth #1: "Fixing weaknesses will create excellence."**
> For individuals and companies, it's a huge mistake to focus all of your attention on fixing your weaknesses. Fixing weaknesses will improve the performance of a person or company, but it will not create greatness. For example, a weakness of many salespeople is record keeping. If you fixed the record-keeping skills of an entire sales force, would you have an excellent sales force? No—at best you would have a better sales force. And if you focused most of your attention on record keeping and neglected the group's sales training, their effectiveness would dwindle. This is the subject of Myth #2.

> **Myth #2: "Talents don't require attention. They take care of themselves."** Traditional thinking says that, if

you want to excel, don't waste your time on improving your talents. Instead, put your time into improving your weak areas. In this case, traditional thinking is wrong.

The cold, hard truth is that everyone can't do everything they set their minds to. People can do outstanding things in areas where they are naturally talented. The trick is to discover your talents and enjoyably use them in your personal life and on the job.

In their book, Clifton and Nelson describe a study on the effectiveness of speed-reading courses. More than a thousand students at the University of Nebraska were evaluated and placed into one of two groups—slow readers and fast readers. Both groups then took a speed-reading course. The slow readers went from an average of ninety words per minute before the course to an average of one hundred and fifty words per minute after the course—a respectable sixty-seven percent increase. To the amazement of the researchers, the fast readers went from an average of 350 words per minute before the course to an average of more than 2,900 words per minute after the course—a 728 percent increase! The moral: talents do require attention to reach their maximum potential.

Myth #3: "Everyone can do anything they set their minds to." Belief in this myth will lead to discouragement and disillusionment because it leads people to believe that they can accomplish anything if they work hard enough at it.

The cold hard truth is that everyone can't do everything they set their minds to. People can do outstanding things in areas where they are naturally talented. The trick is to discover your talents and enjoyable use them in your personal life and on the job.

Use what talents you possess:
the woods would be very silent
if no birds sang except those that sang best.

   —Henry Van Dyke

Discovering Talents

So, how do you discover talents in yourself and others? Here
are four ways.

1. **Pay attention to deeply held desires.** Pinpoint your
   desires. The word *desire* is derived from the Latin word
   desiderare, which means "from the stars." What star
   do you yearn to touch? I'll bet that one of your natural talents is wrapped up in that desire. If you lead or
   manage others, listen for the expression of their desires.
   Then put them in positions where they can express
   their talents.

   You also must watch out for dead-end desires, those
   that make no use of your natural talents but are a byprod-
   uct of them instead. My dead-end desires were money
   and prestige. They led me to dentistry, which didn't play
   to my talents, which in turn led to unhappiness. Other
   dead-end desires are glamour, excitement, and fame. As
   Tiger's life shows, money, prestige, glamour, excitement,
   and fame are all byproducts of fulfilling the deeply held
   desires that are expressions of natural talents.

   Finally, be aware of what others think you should do
   with your life; they may not be considering your talents.
   Too many people are living someone else's visions for
   their lives rather than considering what they're best at

or what their natural talents and desires lead them to do. Make sure the life you live is the one you want. After all, it's the only one you're going to have.

2. **Be alert for fulfillment.** What activities bring you the most fulfillment? What parts of your day seem to fly by and don't feel like work at all? I'll bet a talent is involved in both of these times.

   If you lead or manage people, notice the times when they are fulfilled, and then give them the opportunity to spend more of their time in those activities. This will allow them to soar with their strengths. Everybody—the person, the customer, your company, and you—will win.

3. **Notice rapid learning.** Tiger Woods is the premier example for rapid learning. As you heard earlier, students who were naturally good at reading improved the most when given training. What activities did you learn quickly at any point in your life? A talent was probably in play at that time. At work, what activities do the people you lead or manage pick up quickly? Those activities play to their talents. Have them do more in that area.

To do easily what is difficult for others is the mark of talent.
   —Henri-Frédéric Amiel

4. **Identify snapshots of excellence.** Out of the blue, have you ever done something in a fabulous fashion? Has a person at work done the same? That snapshot of excellence is probably revealing a hidden talent. Capitalize on your discovery.

When it comes to talents, the bottom line is this: Discover what you do best, and then do more of it. In business, discover what the people you lead and manage do best, and then allow them to do more of it. It's also important to realize that a person's talents develop best while on a mission. Tiger's mission in life is to be recognized as the greatest golfer ever as he gives back to the world. What's your mission in life, and how will you harness your talents to live it? What's the mission of your company, and how will you corral the talents of your people to live it?

Discovering Weaknesses

Don't get me wrong—when it comes to weaknesses, I'm not saying that you should never work on them. I am saying that there will come a point in time when the rewards you receive from working on your weaknesses won't be worth your effort. If you're a great manager of people but you're not great at financials, you can work hard to familiarize yourself with basic accounting principles, but there will come a point when learning the details of financial spreadsheets probably will be a waste of your time. The same goes with the people you lead or manage at work. You can offer record-keeping training to your sales staff until you're all blue in the face, but there will come a time when your efforts will be counterproductive.

Weaknesses are painfully easy to detect: Simply review the activities you routinely do and answer these three questions:

1. Is learning this particular activity difficult and slow?

2. Do you dislike doing the activity?

3. Do you feel burned out performing the activity?

If the answer to one or more of the questions is yes, the activity is a weakness for you. You will now need to learn how to manage it.

> *Like all champions, Tiger has the ability to raise his game when he has to. He's not going to burn out because he plays for his own joy and passion.*
>
> —Dr. Jay Brunza

Managing Weaknesses

Your goal is not to ignore your weaknesses. Your goal is to *manage* your weaknesses so your strengths can be unleashed and become so powerful they make the weaknesses irrelevant. Here are four ways to manage a weakness.

1. **Let it go.** This is easier said than done. Sometimes we get stuck in patterns that don't support us. To determine if you should let an activity go, ask yourself these questions:

   - In your personal life and profession, which activities have you done in the last three months that weren't enjoyable?

   - Even though these activities were completed, which of them didn't make a difference in your life? Let these activities go.

2. **Let someone else do it.** When it comes to home repairs and home improvements, I let someone else do it. I don't enjoy doing the repairs and improvements, and I'm not good at it. What activities in your personal and

professional lives fall into the same category? How can you leverage these activities to someone else?

3. **Form partnerships.** The best partnerships are those where the strengths of the people/companies compliment each other. In show business, Cher had singing talent, and Sonny had business talent. Neither of them would probably have made it on their own in the beginning. Tiger Woods is a talented golfer, and his parents are talented at nurturing geniuses. Tiger would have never had the success he is enjoying today if it weren't for the partnership he nurtured with his parents. What partnerships will improve your personal life and business?

4. **Create support systems.** Throughout his golfing career, there has always been a "Team Tiger." At first it was his parents, then the team grew with the addition of a teaching pro, Rudy Duran. Next, sports psychologist Dr. Jay Brunza (quoted on the previous page) was added. The team members have changed through the years, but the goal has remained the same: to create a support system that is designed to maximize Tiger's enormous talent. What support systems do you need in your personal life and profession?

When it comes to weaknesses, the bottom line is this: Discover what you don't do well and stop doing it or do less of it. In business, discover what the people you lead and manage don't do well and allow them to stop doing it, or do less of it.

Maybe you can teach a turkey to climb a tree, but you're probably better off hiring a squirrel in the first place.
　—Kathy Murphy

Beware of the Peter Principle

The Peter Principle is a theory that says employees in an organization will advance to their highest level of competence,
then be promoted to and remain at a level at which they are
incompetent. Why does this happen? One reason can be found
in the study of strengths and weaknesses. For example, Mary
Q. Employee starts at the ABC Company in a position (junior
sales associate) that utilizes her talents. She does well, and she
gets promoted to a higher-level position (senior sales associate) that still utilizes her talents. She continues to do well
and eventually receives a promotion to a higher level (sales
manager). However, this position requires different skills and
doesn't utilize Mary's natural talent for sales. Sales manager
Mary doesn't do well, and therefore she doesn't get promoted.
She remains in the sales manager position for years. Mary
is miserable. The people she manages don't develop as they
should; and her company's bottom line suffers.

The moral: Never promote competent people to positions
that don't utilize their talents. Instead, do your best to find
your people jobs for which their talents are best suited, and
help them grow within those positions.

Realize That Everyone Has a Unique Talent

When Tiger was five, he was regularly shooting in the nineties
for eighteen holes. This caught the attention of the producers
of the TV program *That's Incredible!* He appeared on the show
and flawlessly hit plastic golf balls into the audience, in front
of imposing TV cameras and bright lights—which gave yet
more confidence and poise training to the young superstar.

It would be easy for all this attention at a young age to
go to a child's head, but Earl was determined not to let that

happen. On the same TV program was a ten-year-old girl who showed her unusual strength by lifting the show's three hosts. "Can you do that?" Earl asked Tiger.

"No, Daddy," Tiger replied.

"That's right. She's special in weightlifting and you're special in golf. There are a lot of special people in the world, and you're just one of them. Do you understand that?"

"Yes, Daddy," Tiger said. Earl broke out in goose bumps because he realized that Tiger really did understand.

The lesson Earl taught Tiger at an early age has kept a measured degree of humbleness in the young man who still knows he is one of many special people in the world.

The realization that all members of your business team have natural talents that can be developed with training and experience is a huge advantage for you. If every day you walked past a valuable piece of machinery that was vital to the success of your company, and the machine was running at sixty percent efficiency, what would you do to remedy the situation? Almost anything, right? Many of the people you walk past in your company's hallway each day are like that machine. Their talents aren't being utilized to maximum effectiveness. And it's negatively affecting the profitability of your company far more than a broken piece of machinery.

Imagine what your place would be like if everyone's talents were tapped to the max. They would experience the joy and juice of doing their *best* work, not just *good* work. And your company would reap the rewards. Make talent identification and development an integral part of doing business. Promote it. Reward it. Then, sit back and watch an enthusiastic and talented group of people achieve extraordinary results.

> *One of the greatest talents of all is the talent to recognize and to develop the talents of others.*
> —Frank Tyger

Conclusion

Tiger's phenomenal natural talent was recognized at a very early age by his parents. He steadily developed his talents with the aid of his family and teachers. Through the years, others have come to recognize Tiger's talents. Sportscaster Jim Nantz has said, "He was born to be this poster child—this image of golf." Professional golfer Tom Watson agreed when he remarked, "He is something supernatural." Even Jack Nicklaus, who is generally recognized as the greatest golfer ever, acknowledged Tiger's talent when he proclaimed, "There isn't a flaw in his golf or his makeup. He will win more majors than Arnold Palmer and me combined."

Where do you think Tiger Woods would be today if his natural golfing talent hadn't been identified and developed by Earl and Tida? With such caring parents, I'm sure Tiger would have been successful in whatever he chose to do. But the odds are Tiger would never be in a position similar to the one he enjoys today. You and I would never have come to know and respect him. Tiger would never have been able to influence so many young people. What a waste that would have been.

As you go through life, remember the tale of Tiger's tremendous talents and don't let your talents and the talents of the people you care about go undiscovered and undeveloped.

Your Next Tiger Trait

In Tiger Trait #1, you learned that it's vital to identify and develop your natural talents so you can soar with them. In the next chapter, you will learn how to harness those talents as the "horses" that will pull you toward the clear and compelling dream that you want to create. Read on. Your talents are in the stable and the barn door is open.

TIGER TRAIT#

CREATE A CLEAR AND COMPELLING DREAM

DR. MARTIN LUTHER KING proclaimed, "I have a dream!" He didn't say, "I have a strategic plan." From the very beginning, Walt Disney's dream wasn't to build a company to make cartoons for kids. It was "to use imagination to bring happiness to millions." Mary Kay Ash didn't start Mary Kay Cosmetics to manufacture makeup. She created it to provide business opportunities for women, so that they could go as far as their talents and abilities would take them.

Today, Tiger Woods has a very simple and compelling dream: He wants to be the greatest golfer of all time and to positively affect millions of lives. That's a nice combination because there is something in Tiger's dream for himself and others. Remember that when you crystallize your own dream later in this lesson.

> *Vision is the art of seeing things invisible.*
> —Jonathan Swift

The Power of a Compelling Dream

Compelling dreams are magical. Dreams are like Cinderella's Castle that you see off in the distance as you walk down Main Street in Disneyland or the Magic Kingdom: They mysteriously tug you in their direction. Tiger was never pushed to practice golf. He was pulled to practice by his love of the game and his beckoning dream.

Clear and compelling dreams accomplish three things.

1. **Dreams allow you to use your natural talents to the fullest extent.** Natural talents and dreams are intertwined. You will need one or more of your talents to effectively move toward your dream. Conversely, the creation of a clear and compelling dream will help you identify and develop your talents. Do you see how Tiger's natural talents and dream are linked? Make sure yours are, too.

2. **Dreams identify the path you need to follow.** If you don't have a clear and compelling dream, any old path you're on seems fine. If you do have a clear and compelling dream, and you know your present location in relationship to the dream, then the path to the dream will be vibrantly illuminated for you.

Far away there in the sunshine are my highest aspirations. I may not reach them, but I can look up and see their beauty, believe in them, and follow where they lead.

—Louisa May Alcott

It's vital to be on the right path, because going harder and faster down the wrong path quickly gets you to where you really don't want to be. Early in my career,

I made the "harder and faster" mistake in my dental practice. I thought that more patients, more treatment rooms, more hours at work, and more staff would bring me the success I desired. But all it brought me was more dissatisfaction because I was on the wrong path.

Goals are mileage markers on the path to your dream. When I drive Interstate 15 from Las Vegas to San Diego, there are mileage markers along the way. When I pass them, I know exactly how I'm progressing on my trip. It's the same with goals. In Tiger's case, the goals he has set for himself on his quest to be the greatest golfer of all time will tell him how he's progressing. (You will learn Tiger's goal list in the next chapter.) Moving toward a goal that's not on the path to your dream will have the same effect as moving toward a mileage marker that's not on the road to your destination: It will get you off track even if you do pass it.

Records are meant to be broken. That's why they're made.
—Tiger Woods

3. **Dreams make decision-making easy.** There are many decisions to be made on the path to a dream. When you don't have a clear dream to guide you, decision-making is difficult. When you do have a clear dream to guide you, decision-making is easy. All you have to do is answer this question, "Will this choice move me closer to my dream?" If the answer is yes, and your effort is time- and cost-effective, act on your choice.

There is a very good chance that the choices you make on the path to your dream are not going to be the choices that most people would make. Most people make the popular choices. They do what everybody else does; that's why the majority of them are stuck in the mediocrity quicksand. You're different. You know that the bigger your dream, the more likely you need to make unpopular choices. It goes with the territory.

Before Tiger Woods hit the PGA Tour, the popular choice for professional golfers was very little, if any, physical fitness training. In fact, the prevailing thinking was that weight training decreased your flexibility and ability to hit a golf ball well. Tiger thought differently. With the aid of some very knowledgeable people, he made the unpopular choice and created and implemented a comprehensive weight training, aerobic exercise, and stretching program. I'm sure Tiger would rather be spending his time watching cartoons on TV (he loves them) or honing his skills on the practice tee. But he knows that to reach his dream, he must make unpopular choices. After seeing Tiger's success on the PGA Tour firsthand, most of the other pros adopted physical fitness programs. They had to—Tiger was leaving them in the dust.

Two roads diverged in the wood,
and I— I took the one less traveled by,
And that has made all the difference.
    —Robert Frost

Walt Disney: An American Dreamer

Tiger Woods grew up near the place where the first amusement park was constructed by one of America's most celebrated dreamers, Walt Disney. Walt was born in 1901 in an upstairs bedroom of a small house in Chicago, Illinois. From these humble beginnings he went on to build one of the largest entertainment companies in the world. More important, Walt created a company that is admired worldwide and a cast of characters who are beloved around the globe.

Walt Disney was a dreamer from the very beginning. When he was five years old, his parents and their five children moved to a farm in Marciline, Missouri. Even though Walt lived on the farm for only four years, rural living had a profound effect on his life. On the farm, he was able to get close to many animals that would later become the main characters in his cartoons. He was able to experience the simple life where a child had the time and space to wander and dream. It's easy to imagine Walt on the farm, lying on the grass at night, looking up at the heavens to "wish upon a star," just like the song Jiminy Cricket sang in *Pinocchio*. Forty years later, when Walt built a workshop on his estate in California, it was an exact replica of the barn he remembered in Marciline. Walt had a way of turning dreams into realities.

When he was in grade school, his fourth grade teacher instructed the class to draw the bowl of flowers on her desk. Walt drew the flowers with faces on them and transformed the leaves into arms! His teacher was not pleased. Even then, people who thought differently were put down. Luckily, Walt didn't pay much attention to the naysayers. He was too busy expressing his talents.

No great artist sees things as they really are.
If he did, he would cease to be an artist.
    —Oscar Wilde

In Kansas City, Walt had a small cartoon company that failed. (Contrary to popular opinion, dreamers don't have fewer failures. They just learn from their experiences and keep moving.) He decided to start over in Hollywood. To raise money for the train ticket, he went door to door, photographing babies. He left Kansas City wearing a checkered coat and pants that didn't match. He had $40 in cash. His imitation leather suitcase contained one shirt, two pairs of undershorts, two pairs of socks, and some drawing materials. But when he paid for his fare, he bought a first-class ticket. Walt Disney had a dream. He knew where he was going. He wanted to arrive in style.

> *When you believe in a thing,*
> *believe in it implicitly and unquestionably.*
> —Walt Disney

In Hollywood, Walt had his share of successes and failures, but his dream to use imagination to bring happiness to millions never died. As a result of that dream, the world viewed its first talking cartoon, *Steamboat Willie*, starring Mickey Mouse, and its first full-length feature cartoon, *Snow White*.

In the early 1950s, Walt's dream expanded. He wanted to create an amusement park like no other. His business associates thought he was crazy. They told him, "We're in the movie business, not the amusement park business." Walt replied, "We're in the *happiness* business. Disneyland will bring more happiness to millions of people in ways that movies never could." Sometimes dreamers have to ignore the misgivings of those around them. It goes with the territory.

Walt's preliminary drawings for Disneyland were put in a folder with the following description.

The idea of Disneyland is a simple one. It will be a place for people to find happiness and knowledge. It will be a place for parents and children to share pleasant times in one another's company: a place for teachers and pupils to discover greater ways of understanding and education. Here the older generation can recapture the nostalgia of days gone by and the younger generation can savor the challenge of the future. Here will be the wonders of Nature and Man for all to see and understand.

Disneyland will be based upon and dedicated to the ideals, the dreams, and the hard facts that have created America. And it will be uniquely equipped to dramatize these dreams and facts and send them forth as a source of courage and inspiration to the entire world.

Disneyland will be a fair, an exhibition, a playground, a community center, a museum of living facts, and a showplace of beauty and magic. It will be filled with the accomplishments, the joys, and the hopes of the world we live in. And it will remind us and show us how to make those wonders a part of our own lives. Sometime in 1955, Walt Disney will present for the people of the world—and children of all ages—a new experience in entertainment.

How's that for a vivid and compelling description of a dream? Do you see how a dream like that would attract people and resources? Do you see how a dream like that would provide the enthusiasm and commitment to keep going down the path even when things are tough? Do you now see that you need a dream like this for your own life and business? I hope so. So let's create a vivid and compelling dream description for your life and/or business right now.

As you create your dream, don't be realistic. Being realistic deals with the world as it is right now. That's not where you want to be in ten years. Instead of being realistic, be futuristic. Be a dreamer.

> *A dream is a wish your heart makes.*
> —Jiminy Cricket

Create Your Compelling Dream

In the next chapter, you'll learn how, at the age of ten, Tiger saw a list in *Golf Digest* of Jack Nicklaus' accomplishments on the golf course and the ages at which he achieved them. Tiger clipped the list and posted it in his room. At the tender age of ten, Tiger's dream was to be the best golfer ever. His dream provided the emotional fuel that pulled him in its direction. The list became his goals on the path to the dream. Tiger's natural talents provided the vehicle. His uncompromising work ethic has kept him relentlessly on the road.

Right now, pull out a piece of paper and write a two- or three-paragraph description of the life of your dreams. Include both your personal life and business. Before you start writing, take another look at what Walt wrote about Disneyland (you'll find the description on page 27.) Notice how many times he used the word be. Also notice the number of times Walt talked about what Disneyland would give its visitors. You should do the same with the description of your compelling dream. Be sure to include a healthy dose of the person you will be and the gifts you will give. Most people focus on the activities they want to do and the material possessions they want to have. Those are important, too, but they will come to you only when you're being the right person and giving the right gifts. We will talk more about *be, do, have,* and *give* in the last chapter.

If you are in a leadership position at work, write a two- or three-paragraph description of the business of your dreams. Be sure you describe what the business will be and what it will give your customers/clients.

> *We are told never to cross a bridge until we come to it,*
> *but this world is owned by people who have crossed*
> *bridges in their imaginations far ahead of the crowd.*
> —Andrew Fitzpatrick

Influence Others to Buy into Your Dream

Creating a compelling dream for your business is the first step. After all, you gotta have a dream to make a dream come true. Rarely can you make your dream come true without the help of other people. In the case of creating the business of your dreams, you're going to have to influence the people at work to buy into your dream. If you can't do this effectively, you're setting yourself up for discouragement and failure. When you do this now, you will "grease the wheels" of your success.

Throughout his life, Tiger Woods has influenced people to assist him in the attainment of his dream. (You'll meet many of them in Tiger Trait #3, "Select Teachers, Heroes, and Teammates Who Guide, Inspire, and Support.")

In 1952, Walt Disney had to influence his board members to approve the Disneyland project. It wasn't easy. He told them passionately, "There's nothing like it in the entire world. I know, because I've looked. That's why it can be great; because it will be unique, a new concept in entertainment. And I think—I *know*—it can be a success." When Walt finished speaking, there were tears in his eyes. The members of the board were persuaded and approved the project.

You've got to do the same with the key people in your life. But you must begin with *you*. In order to influence other people, you've got to be influenced first. That's why having a crystal-clear and compelling dream is so important. The emotion generated every time you think of your dream will flow into your words and body language so that people will think, "This person really believes in what she's talking about! She's going to make it happen. I want to be on the bandwagon."

> *Many hands, and hearts, and minds generally contribute to anyone's notable achievements.*
> —Walt Disney

You need to sit down with your people at work and convincingly convey the following:

- Exactly what your dream is
- Why the dream is so important to you
- What's in it for them? How will they benefit? How will helping you achieve your dream move them closer to their dreams?
- What you expect from them
- A simple plan for the achievement of the dream
- A call to action. In the story above, Walt asked for the loan. You should do the same.

> *The growth and development of the Walt Disney Company is directly related to the growth and development of its human resources—our cast.*
> —Walt Disney

Mental Creation Precedes Physical Creation

Walt Disney died before Disney World in Orlando was completed. His brother, Roy, came out of retirement and finished the project. On the opening day of Disney World, a young reporter came up to Roy and said, "Isn't it a tragedy that Walt never got to see Walt Disney World?" Roy Disney replied, "You're wrong, young man. Walt did see it. He saw it in his imagination first. That's why you're seeing it physically here today."

Walt Disney practiced the art of creating reality in his mind first. Tiger Wood learned the same lesson very early in his life. At the age of six, he won the ten-and-under division of the Optimist World Junior championship. After the tournament was over, Earl asked Tiger what he was thinking about on the first tee. "Where I wanted the ball to go, Daddy," he replied. At six years old, Tiger knew that mental creation precedes physical creation—the vision precedes the reality.

Even today, before each shot Tiger takes on the golf course or practice range, he sees the perfect shot in his mind's eye. Then he steps up to the ball and physically re-creates the mental image. He does the same thing with his future by mentally creating it in advance. When you adopt this Tiger Trait, the mental "acorn" of your vision will turn into the mighty oak of your realized dream.

> *The greatest achievement was at first and for a time a dream.*
> *The oak sleeps in the acorn, the bird waits in the egg,*
> *and in the highest vision of the soul, a waking angel stirs.*
> *Dreams are the seedlings of realities.*
> —James Allen

Your Next Tiger Trait

Now that you've learned how to identify and develop your natural talents and created a compelling dream, it's time to select the people who will guide, inspire, and support you. Tiger and his parents were masters at this. In a few minutes, you will be, too. In chapter 3 you will learn how to select teachers, heroes, and teammates who will guide, inspire, and support you.

TIGER TRAIT#

SELECT TEACHERS, HEROES, AND TEAMMATES WHO GUIDE, INSPIRE, AND SUPPORT

THE MOST MEMORABLE EVENT in the Tiger Woods' career to date started on Sunday, April 13, 1997, at 2:50 P.M. on the first tee of the Augusta National Golf Club. The millions viewing the televised live broadcast made this Masters golf tournament the most watched golfing event in history. Thousands lined the first tee, fairway, and green. Among them were Tida and Earl Woods.

As Tiger teed off on that first hole, he was also teeing off a new era for golf—an era that could include more people of all races, economic backgrounds, and ages. For the moment, Tiger Woods was a symbol of other people's dreams. He had won the Masters in his imagination hundreds of times. He was about to see if he could win it in reality on his first attempt as a professional golfer.

Even though Tiger was standing on that first tee all by himself that day, there were millions of people who were beside him in spirit. The most notable of these were Tiger's teachers, heroes, and teammates—the people who helped him become the person on the center stage that day. The next few pages profile these people and the ways Tiger has benefited from them being in his life.

The Teachers: Those Who Guide

Earl and Tida Woods

While on duty in Bangkok, Thailand, Earl met a pretty young woman named Tida who worked as a secretary in the Army office. They fell in love, moved to the U.S., and were married in Brooklyn, New York, in 1969. After Earl accepted a position at McDonnell Douglas in 1975, they relocated to Cypress, California. On December 30th of that year, a baby boy, Eldrick, was born to the couple. The first letter of Eldrick represents Earl, and the last letter represents Kultida. His parents created this unusual first name to constantly remind Tiger that he is always surrounded by his parents' love.

As you learned earlier, Earl was the first person to catch a glimpse of Tiger's genius when the toddler was ten months old. Luckily, Earl knew it would take more than natural ability for Tiger to fulfill his potential. It would also take a team of support people, a passion for excellence that only a compelling dream can ignite, and countless hours of practice. Earl knew that, like a growing plant, genius evolves best when it's nurtured—when it's allowed to gradually mature and bloom at the appropriate time.

On many occasions, Earl has expressed the belief that his life experiences were given to him by a higher power to prepare him to be Tiger's father. He said, "I truly believe that without the many obstacles I have faced in my own life—from poverty to racism to near-death in war—I could not have raised the son you see before you today."

Because of Earl's modest income and the couple's decision to have Tida stay home with Tiger (he never had a babysitter), Tida and Earl didn't take a vacation in over twenty years while raising Tiger. They spent between $25,000 and $30,000 a year to enter Tiger in national tournaments and to travel with him. While Earl and Tida weren't financially rich, they were rich in more important areas: the ideals, beliefs, and standards they held dear. They instilled these building blocks of success in Tiger so he could become the person he is today.

Here are five of those ideals, beliefs, and standards.

1. **Family first, homework second, golf third.** This was one of Tida's unbreakable rules. Tiger was never allowed to practice until his homework was completed. And family time always came first.

2. **Try your best.** When Tiger was six years old, he played with a club professional named Stewart Reed. Tiger was beating Reed after the first nine holes, but eventually lost on the second nine. Tiger left the course in tears and refused to shake Reed's hand after the round was over. "You must be a sportsman, win or lose," his mom scolded him. Even though Tiger was a winner more often than not, he was never chastised or forced to practice more when he did lose. His parents knew and communicated that winning was important, but not all-important.

   You try your best. That's all I need to hear from you. You try your best.
       —Tida Woods

3. **Be humble and respectful.** With the benefit of her Asian upbringing, Tida was the primary instiller of this ideal.

Tiger continually acknowledges the debt to his parents and all the other people who helped him along the way. Even though he's the best in the world at what he does, Tiger keeps his feet on the ground and always respects his teachers, fellow professionals, and other members of his team.

4. **Share and care.** Tida and Earl were the perfect parents for Tiger. Both of them made raising Tiger their number-one priority. Each of them infused their son with the ideals, beliefs, and standards they held dear. Sharing and caring were two of Earl's priorities, and he has instilled those values into his son.

5. **Let your clubs speak for you.** Sadly, the entire Woods family and even young Tiger were the targets of racial bigotry on numerous occasions on and off the golf course. When this happened to Tiger, his mother would say, "When you've been wronged, when you've been angered, don't say or do anything. Let your clubs speak for you." In Tiger Trait #6, you will learn more about this action orientation.

As you've seen, Tiger has two very unusual and complementary parents. His mother instilled in Tiger the basic philosophies of the Eastern cultures. His dad, a former Green Beret with a never-say-die attitude, made sure that Tiger had the mental, physical and technical training that no other golfer ever had. Tida coined the term "Team Tiger" to represent the ever-changing group of people whose task it was to teach, inspire, and support Tiger in his quest to become the best golfer ever. In this chapter you'll learn about the people who have been part of Team Tiger, helping to hone Tiger's exceptional talent and shape his life and career.

Earl Woods died on May 3, 2006, and Tiger took a month off from playing in tournaments. After Tiger won the 2006 British Open on July 23, he embraced his caddy, Steve Williams, and sobbed uncontrollably. Steve whispered in his ear, "This one's for Pops."

Rudy Duran

In his book, *In Every Kid There Lurks a Tiger,* Rudy Duran described how Tida walked into his pro shop with Tiger, and asked Rudy to give her four-year-old son lessons. Rudy was doubtful, but he took Tiger out to the golf range. The little boy hit several golf balls perfectly. Rudy told Tida he'd be happy to teach Tiger, and he did for six years.

Rudy was a master at instructing young golfers. Here's what he said and his teaching philosophies and Tiger:

> When I first saw him at four years old, it was unbelievable. There he was smacking balls like a pro. He was a genius like Einstein or Mozart. What he needed to know from me were the basic things about golf and the rules. Then, he needed to be assured that he was doing everything correctly. When he was doing something well, there was plenty of praise. When something wasn't right, I didn't criticize but just gave him the right information, so he could process the information and execute it. ...I knew he was going to be a superstar from the beginning.

In the next Tiger Trait, you will learn how Rudy enhanced Tiger's confidence by creating a special "Tiger par" for each hole he played.

Dr. Jay Brunza

Jay Brunza was a Navy captain and clinical psychologist who regularly played with Earl on the Navy golf courses. In a *USA Today* article in July 1992, Dr. Brunza wrote, "Tiger is so advanced mentally, it's scary. I did some sports psychology with athletes at the Naval Academy where we worked on things like ways to focus attention, and Tiger is far ahead of anything I've ever seen."

Dr. Fran Pirozzolo, a sports psychologist for the New York Yankees baseball team, says, "Tiger has no equal when it comes to mental focus. Tiger plays within a shell of concentration that cracks open only after he wins the championship he's playing in, usually by a record score." You will learn more about mental focus in Tiger Trait #5.

John Anselmo

John Anselmo became Tiger's teaching professional when Tiger was ten. He continued to instruct Tiger until he was eighteen. In addition to assisting Tiger with his physical game, John enhanced Tiger's mental game by instilling thoughts such as

- "Don't try hard. Try to be fluid."
- "The ball is not to be hit. It is to be directed."
- "Hit with your practice swing."

John also taught Tiger these mental strategies.

- Instead of looking down at the ball, he instructed Tiger to look through the ball from back to front and then down the target line. This mental process enabled Tiger to do a better job of powerfully swinging through the ball.

- To ensure Tiger would hit his putts hard enough on slow greens or uphill putts, John would have him hit to an imaginary hole a few feet past the real one.

- To allow Tiger to ignore a water hazard in front of a green, John would have Tiger imagine the colorful flag at the top of the flagstick and aim for that.

(Reread the previous six bullet points, and notice how each one applies to the game of golf *and* the game of life.)

Mark O'Meara

In Tom Callahan's book, *In Search of Tiger*, Tiger describes his relationship with professional golfer, Mark O'Meara in this way: "He kind of took me aside and showed me the ropes of life away from college, life on your own. Sometimes I miss college. Miss just hanging around. Drinking beer. Talking half the night. Getting in a little trouble. Being with people my own age. You come home to your house and no one's there. How do you get over the loneliness factor of playing and practicing so much golf? Marko basically opened up his arms and his house to me and said, 'Come be a part of our family.'" Mark has become a kind of big brother to Tiger, advising him on everything from agents to coaches to hobbies.

Sometimes it's difficult to determine who is the teacher and who is the student. Mark O'Meara is almost twenty years older than Tiger. Like Tiger, he won his own U.S. Amateur title in 1979. By most standards, O'Meara was successful: He had won over $10 million dollars on the tour. But before meeting Tiger, Mark was winless in fifty-six major tournaments. After he met Tiger, at the age of forty-one, Mark won his first major—the Masters in 1998. A proud friend and defending champion, Tiger Woods, slipped the Masters green jacket on Mark at the winner's ceremony.

> *No matter how tough we think we are, we can't do it alone.*
> —Tiger Woods

Butch Harmon

When Tiger was seventeen years old, Earl selected teaching professional Butch Harmon to take his son's game to the next level. "He's the best student I ever had," Butch later remarked. "He's like a sponge—he soaks up information and he always wants to learn and get better."

Butch worked with Tiger on the mental and physical aspects of the game. In Tiger Trait #2, "Create a Clear and Compelling Dream," you learned that mental creation pre-cedes physical creation. Butch taught Tiger the "eyes shut, open mind" drill that harnessed the power of mental creation. Butch had Tiger mentally experience in great detail the move-ments of his body and club as he executed a perfect swing. Then, with Tiger's eyes closed, Butch had him actually hit the ball. The vast majority of the time, Tiger did it flawlessly.

Hank Haney

Sometimes, the teacher who gets you from point A to point B isn't the best teacher to get you to point C. In the spring of 2004, on the advice of Mark O'Meara, Tiger switched swing coaches and started working with Texan Hank Haney. Hank wanted to keep the relationship quiet because he knew the experts (i.e., every golfer in the world) would be questioning the changes Tiger made in his swing. He was right. Tiger didn't win a major tournament in his next ten attempts. But the changes have paid off in spades as evidenced by Tiger's victories at the 2005 Masters, the 2005 and 2006 British Opens, and the 2006 PGA Championship.

The Heroes: Those Who Inspire

Nguyen Phong

In the late 1960s, former Green Beret/U.S. Army lieutenant colonel Earl Woods was walking along a rice paddy dike in Vietnam. All was quiet until a voice yelled out, "Get down, Woody!" Earl quickly dove for cover. A moment later, a barrage of bullets filled the space he had just vacated.

About twenty minutes later, when they were out of the sniper's range, Earl curled up in a bamboo thicket to catch some much-needed zzzz's. After he dozed off, Earl heard the same voice again. "Don't move, Woody. There's a bamboo viper about two inches from your right eye." Earl looked to the right and gazed into the eyes of the venomous snake. His survival depended on absolute stillness. Being the battled-tested Green Beret he was, Earl passed the test. The snake slithered away.

Both times, the voice that saved Earl Woods life was that of Nguyen Phong, a lieutenant colonel in the South Vietnamese Army. "He was special," Earl later related. "He was a tiger in combat, so I began calling him Tiger." Earl vowed that, if he ever had a son, he would call the boy Tiger. Earl returned to the States in 1971. Four years later Saigon fell to the communists. Earl never heard from Phong again. Over thirty years later, he learned that Phong died in 1976 in a North Vietnamese prison camp.

In his fantastic book, *In Search of Tiger,* Tom Callahan retells a conversation he had with Tiger Woods.

> **Tiger:** "I always knew there was another Tiger.
> I didn't know him as Tiger Phong. I just knew
> him as Tiger One."

Then Tom asked Tiger if he felt a connection to Tiger One.

> **Tiger:** "A stronger one than I can explain to you.
> From all I hear, I'm exactly like him. It's an honor
> to have his name."

Jack Nicklaus

Most golfers believe that Jack Nicklaus is the best to ever play the game. When Tiger was ten years old, he took a list of Jack's golfing accomplishments that had been published in *Golf Digest* and posted it in his room. Over the next eleven years, every time he accomplished a golfing milestone on Jack's list, Tiger would write how old he was when he did the same. Here is a partial list comparing the two men:

- Jack was nine when he first shot under fifty for nine holes. Tiger was three.

- Jack was twelve when he first shot under eighty for eighteen holes. Tiger was eight.

- Jack was thirteen when he first broke seventy. Tiger was twelve.

- Jack was nineteen when he won his first U.S. Amateur championship. Tiger was eighteen.

- Jack was twenty-two when he won his first major professional championship. Tiger was twenty-one.

- Jack won his fiftieth PGA event at the age of thirty-three years and six months. Tiger won his fiftieth at thirty years, seven months.

- Jack was thirty when he won his eighth major professional championship. At thirty, Tiger had won twelve.

Jack and Tiger are similar in their golfing achievements and, more important, they are similar in their approaches to life. The following two quotes from Tiger, reported in Tom Callahan's book, illustrate what I mean:

> If you aspire to greatness, you have to have a clear picture of greatness. Jack and I have an understanding of each other, just because of the way we play. The passion and the competitive drive we both have—it's inherent. I definitely sense something when I'm around him. We're a lot alike.
>
> The weird thing is that I've had several lunches with him, and I've talked with him on the golf course. But we've never once talked about playing golf. You'd think I'd try to pick his brain, wouldn't you? But I already know what he'd say. It's like we both know what we both know. There's no need to put words to it.

The respect between Jack and Tiger is mutual. Here's what Jack has said about his records and Tiger Woods: "Somebody is going to dust my records. It might as well be Tiger because he's such a great kid."

Even though Tiger used Jack Nicklaus' accomplishments as a scorecard for his own career, he never tried to copy any one golfer. As Tiger has said, "I've tried to adopt the best attributes of many people. I've always studied great players. They were great for a reason. More important, I like to study their decision-making on the golf course. I've tried to pick fifty players and combine the best of them, and make one great player."

I use not only all the brains I have, but all I can borrow.
—Woodrow Wilson

Charlie Sifford

Tiger looked up to Charlie Sifford, the greatest of golf's black pioneers. In the 1950s, when Charlie was in his prime, the Professional Golfers Association (PGA) limited its membership to "professional golfers of the Caucasian race." In the 1960s, Charlie won two PGA events, but he still was not invited to the Masters Tournament that year. When Tiger won the Masters in 1997, a seventy-six-year-old Charlie Sifford said, "As far as I'm concerned, it puts the Masters to rest for me."

If I have seen further,
it is by standing on the shoulders of giants.
—Sir Isaac Newton

Nelson Mandela

On a trip to a tournament in South Africa, Tiger and Earl paid a visit to one of their heroes, Nelson Mandela, at his summer home. In *In Search of Tiger*, by Tom Callahan, Earl Woods relates the following story: "He (Mandela) and Tiger instantly locked eyes. They knew each other immediately. They began to talk, to communicate. I just watched, amazed. I couldn't believe the ease they both felt in each other's presence. It was like a teacher and his best student. It was beautiful. 'You have this ability,' Nelson told him. 'Do some good with it.' "

Tiger has followed his hero's advice. He has taken his natural golf ability and his acquired role-model status and done some good with it. You will learn more about "the good" in Tiger Trait #9, "Be Grateful. Give Back."

The Teammates: Those Who Support

Elin Nordegren Woods

Tiger met his future wife in 2001 while she was working as a nanny for pro golfer Jesper Parnevik's kids. They were married in 2004. One observer calls her the "Greta Garbo of tour wives" because she wears dark Nike apparel as she watches Tiger play, and she keeps a low profile. When asked if she would ever run onto the green after a Tiger victory and give him a kiss, she replied, "Oh, no, never." Tiger showed how much he appreciates her support when he said, "Without a doubt, it helps having a partner there. We're like a team. It makes you stronger."

Steve Williams

Tiger's caddie, Steve Williams, is good-natured off the course, but, like Tiger, when he walks onto the first tee, he is all business. Steve will do almost anything to protect Tiger's safety and concentration. The best example is when he threw a photographer's camera into a lake at the 2002 Merrill Lynch Skins Game when the guy snapped a shot during Tiger's backswing. A native of New Zealand, Steve is as competitive as his boss. Steve says, "Between the two of us, it's a bit of a battle.

I thought I was a competitive person until I met him, and that meeting certainly turned a lot of corners in my life."

Hudeyuki "Rock" Ishii

Rock is probably the least known Team Tiger member. He is the creator of all Tiger's Nike golf balls. In 2000, Tiger began using one of Rock's solid core balls. A few months later, he won the U.S. Open at Pebble Beach by fifteen strokes. Tiger told *Sports Illustrated*, "Rock is incredible. He can take what I'm feeling and transfer it into numbers, and those numbers become technology." To this day, Rock inspects every ball delivered to Tiger.

Mark Steinberg

In 1960, Mark McCormack shook hands with a young golfer named Arnold Palmer. That historic handshake marked the beginning of the legendary sports and lifestyle marketing and management company, IMG. One of IMG's senior vice presidents, Mark Steinberg, has been in charge of "brand Tiger" since 1998. Here's what Mark told a Wharton College audience in 2003: "Coca-Cola, Kodak, Nike, those are three of the largest international brands. Tiger Woods is on par with them." Mark convinced Tiger to endorse Buick, to the benefit of both: Buick has dramatically upgraded its image, and Tiger collects a cool $6 million a year.

The 1997 Masters Tournament

In the beginning of this chapter, we left Tiger as he was standing on the first tee of the Augusta National Golf Club in Augusta, Georgia. On the front nine of the opening round, he shot a very un-Tiger-like four over par score of forty. On the back nine, he righted the ship with a six under par thirty. That gave him a score of seventy for the day—good enough for fourth place, three strokes behind the leader.

On the second day, Tiger shot the day's best score of sixty-six, which gave him a three-stroke lead at the halfway point of the tournament. On day three, Tiger had eleven pars and seven birdies for a round of sixty-five, stretching his lead to nine strokes. On the final round, with 15.3 million homes watching on television, Tiger shot a sixty-nine. His eighteen-under-par score of 270 for the tournament was a record, as was his winning margin of twelve strokes. At twenty-one he was the youngest player ever to win the Masters. And he was the first person of color ever to win a major tournament.

After he sank his four-foot par putt on the eighteenth hole, television announcer Jim Nantz summed up the moment when he said, "There it is—a win for the ages." Then, with the TV cameras following his every move, Tiger embraced the two most important people in his life—his dad and mom. His dad wasn't supposed to be there as he had recently undergone coronary bypass surgery. President Clinton called Tiger later in the evening and said the embrace with Earl was the best shot he saw on TV all day.

Here's how Earl described the moment (from *Tiger: The Authorized DVD Collection*).

"You're not very often afforded the privilege of seeing your child make history. I don't know how many volts of electricity went between us. Time stood still. It was just he and I. And we just loved and loved and loved some more. There wasn't anything I could do. I was so proud of him. The love we have for each other—it just flowed."

A few minutes later, Tiger gave his acceptance speech on the eighteenth green (from *Tiger: The Authorized DVD Collection*). Here's how he described the scene.

> "When I won, to stand there on that green and give my speech. It was pretty cool just to look back on the clubhouse and see all the porters, all the cooks and everybody back there who was of color come out to watch my speech. That's special. That's very special."

One of the great traditions is the awarding of the green jacket to the winner of the Masters. Tiger Woods wore his jacket proudly at the champion's dinner that night. He was wearing it for himself, his parents, his teachers, his heroes, and the millions of people who believed in him. Later that evening, during a celebration party in a house Tiger had rented for his stay at the Masters, Tida Woods noticed her son was missing. She went to an upstairs bedroom and found Tiger fast asleep, clutching that green jacket like it was a teddy bear.

Conclusion

In addition to answering the questions below, you may want to reread this chapter—this time with an eye toward identifying the key lessons you can apply in your personal life and business.

1. Who guides, inspires, and supports you in your personal life and business? Who will you add to the lists?

2. Who do you guide, inspire, and support in your personal life and business? How will you then do a better job of guiding, inspiring, and supporting?

Your Next Tiger Trait

Do you see how each Tiger Trait builds on the previous one? First, you identify and develop your natural talents. Then you create a clear and compelling dream that utilizes your natural talents. Next, you select the teachers, heroes, and teammates who guide, inspire, and support. When you've done that, you need to be confident as you move toward your dream. Confidence is the fascinating subject of the next lesson. Don't be shy. Flip the page and take your next step.

To discover Tiger Trait #10, go to
www.tigertraitsbookbonus.com now.

TIGER TRAIT# 4

BE CONFIDENT

FROM THE VERY BEGINNING, Tiger had a simple goal for each tournament he entered: to win. Not everybody had that much confidence in him, as is shown by the following exchange between Tiger and ABC broadcaster Curtis Strange. This conversation occurred in 1996, right before Tiger's first professional tournament, the Milwaukee Open.

Strange: What would make a successful week here in Milwaukee?

Tiger: If I can play four solid rounds. And a victory would be awfully nice, too.

Strange: A victory? To me that comes off as a little cocky or brash. Especially talking to, you know, the other guys who have been out here for years and years and years. And, you know, certainly an incredible amateur record—but what do you say to those guys when you come out here? You know what I'm saying? You come out here, your first pro tournament, and say, "I can win"?

Tiger: I understand. But I've always figured, why go to a tournament if you're not going there to try to win? There's really no point even going. That's the attitude I've had my entire life. That's the attitude I'll always have. As I would explain to my dad, second sucks, and third is worse. That's just a belief I have.

Strange: But on tour that's not too bad.

Tiger: That's not too bad. But I want to win. That's just my nature.

Strange: (laughing) You'll learn.

Making the Unreasonable Reasonable

What Curtis was trying to convey to Tiger was that, from his perspective, it was unreasonable for Tiger to expect to win his first professional tournament. But being reasonable isn't all that it's cracked up to be. As Samuel Butler said, "The reasonable man adapts himself to the world, but the unreasonable man tries to adapt the world to him—therefore, all progress depends upon the unreasonable man." Tiger hasn't learned to be reasonable. He hasn't lowered his expectations. He has maintained his confidence and has achieved "unreasonable" accomplishments on and off the golf course.

One definition of confidence is "the positive expectation of a favorable outcome." As his conversation with Curtis Strange illustrates, Tiger Woods has a positive expectation of a favorable outcome every time he enters a tournament. He's said that his only purpose for playing golf is to win, and he believes that he shares that winning mindset with most champions. "You have to adopt a no-fear attitude," he has said. While this attitude may seem arrogant to some, to Tiger it simply represents his honest approach to the game.

Tiger's confidence is not an accident. It's the culmination of an abundance of natural talent, a dream requiring excellence to achieve, and a team of people who build confidence by guiding, inspiring, and supporting. Throughout the years, Team Tiger has provided oodles of confidence-building instruction and experience for Tiger. Below are some examples.

His Parents' Early Advice

Much of Tiger's confidence was instilled at an early age by his parents. In the last Tiger Trait, you learned how the unique blend of Tida's Eastern and Earl's Western cultures came together with their commitment to raise a child who excelled on the golf course and in life. Confidence is one of the many attributes the pair instilled in Tiger, as Earl's following three comments illustrate:

"I knew he would be the best in the world."

"When you're on the golf course, you're the boss."

"'Tiger, I promise you one thing. You'll never meet another person as tough as you.' He hasn't, and he never will."

Tiger Par

In the last chapter, you learned that Rudy Duran was Tiger's first professional teacher when Tiger was four through ten years old. Rudy established a "Tiger par" for each hole the child played. If Tiger reached a green with four perfect shots,

Rudy made Tiger par for that hole a six—four to reach the green plus two putts. This kind of thinking was vital to Tiger's success. He had something to shoot for on every hole—something he could attain with excellent execution. From the very beginning, the young golfer rarely shot over "Tiger par." This allowed him to gain confidence at a very young age—a trademark of Tiger's tournament play in later years.

*Have confidence that if you have done a little thing well,
you can do a bigger thing well, too.*
—Joseph Storey

Gaining Confidence at the U.S. Amateur Championships

As you discovered in Tiger Trait #3, Tiger won three consecutive U.S. Junior Amateur Championships—a feat never before accomplished. In the three years after that, Tiger captured three consecutive U.S. Amateur Championships. No one has ever done that either—not Bobby Jones, considered the best amateur ever to play the game, and not Jack Nicklaus. The U.S. Amateur Championship is an especially difficult tournament to win because it is open to all U.S. citizens of any age who aren't golf professionals. In addition, the road to the winner's circle is long and difficult. Only the best golfers qualify for the first two rounds of stroke play. The sixty-four lowest scores qualify for six rounds of match play.* The first five match play

---

*In match play golf, you only compete against one opponent. If you shoot a lower score on a hole than your opponent, you receive one point. The player who collects the most points wins the match.

rounds are eighteen holes each, and the final round is thirty-six holes, all played in one day.

Tiger's U.S. Amateur Championship #1

The 1994 U.S. Amateur Championship was held at the Stadium Course at the Tournament Players Club at Sawgrass in Ponte Vedra, Florida. When eighteen-year-old Tiger Woods stepped on the fourteenth tee for the last round of his first U.S. Amateur Championship, it didn't look like he would be stepping into the history book. His opponent, Trip Kuehne, birdied seven of the first thirteen holes to take a six-hole lead. No one had ever come from that far behind to win the U.S. Amateur, and no one that young had ever won the U.S. Amateur. At the end of the first eighteen holes, Tiger was still four holes down.

As Tiger approached the first tee for the final round, Earl pulled him aside and whispered in his ear, "Son, let the legend grow." And grow it did. After being down by five holes with twelve holes to play, Tiger won the match and the championship on the final hole.

Would Tiger have won if Earl hadn't whispered his five-word confidence-booster? Who knows for sure? One thing that is for sure—Earl knew how to say the right thing at the right time.

Tiger's U.S. Amateur Championship #2

In his second U.S. Amateur Championship, Tiger played poorly the first two days of stroke play, barely making the cut. In spite of this, Tiger displayed his usual candor and confidence. "I'm extremely disappointed. I don't know what went wrong. But I should get it squared away in fifteen minutes of practice," he said. The practice paid off. He went on to win six straight one-on-one matches and the title.

Tiger's U.S. Amateur Championship #3

After his first round victory in match play, Tiger, Jay Brunza, and a friend went to the movie *Tin Cup*. *Tin Cup* is about an underdog golfer who defies the odds, takes tremendous risk, and has his moment of glory. On the way back to their hotel, the threesome stopped at the course where Tiger had won his third U.S. Junior Championship. All three men knew that golfers draw confidence from visualizing outstanding shots from their past, so they walked to a sand trap on the eighteenth hole where Tiger had hit one of the most dramatic shots of his career. The shot had landed eight feet from the hole; Tiger had made the putt and won the tournament. As he stood by that sand trap three years later, with his two buddies by his side, Tiger replayed the shot in his mind, thereby creating the additional confidence he needed to continue the quest for his third consecutive U.S. Amateur Championship the next day.

As it turned out, Tiger needed all the confidence he could get. In the match play finals, he trailed his opponent, Steve Scott, by five holes with eighteen holes to go. Two years before, in a similar situation, Earl had told his son, "Let the legend grow." This time he decided not to say anything. Earl knew Tiger had grown to the point where he could handle the situation himself.

By the tenth hole, Tiger had cut Scott's lead to one. But with three holes remaining, Tiger trailed by two. He made a birdie on the sixteenth hole to pull to within one. Then he made a thirty-foot birdie putt on seventeen to tie the match. Tiger and Scott tied the eighteenth hole, sending the match into a sudden-death playoff. Tiger won his third consecutive

U.S. Amateur Championship on the second playoff hole. Later, he had this to say about his three U.S. Amateur Championships in a row: "The greatest players ever, Nicklaus and Jones, never did this. I like to be unique, to accomplish things that have never been done."

A new chapter in Tiger's life began the very next day. He flew to Milwaukee on a Nike corporate jet to play in his first professional tournament.

The Power of Confidence

In *Confidence: How Winning Streaks and Losing Streaks Begin and End*, Rosabeth Moss Kanter says, "Confidence lies at the heart of civilization. Everything about an economy, a society, and organization or a team depends on it. Every step we take, every investment we make, is based on whether we feel we can count on ourselves and others to accomplish what has been promised. Confidence determines whether our steps—individually and collectively—are tiny and tentative or big and bold."

As you learned earlier, confidence is the positive expectation of a favorable outcome. Confidence must be experienced in appropriate doses. Over-confidence by a person or group leads to cockiness. If Tiger were over-confident, he would sabotage his future success by being satisfied with his mental and technical skills. He wouldn't put in enough time on the practice tee and green. He would become complacent with his physical fitness program. He would underestimate his opponents' ability to win. The same is true with businesses—they, too, become fat and happy. Ten years ago big airlines like United, American, and Delta ruled the skies. Today, they are fighting for survival.

Under-confidence is just as bad, because it can leads to cowardice. If Tiger were under-confident, he wouldn't take the calculated risks that produce championships. He would fall apart when the going got tough. His opponents would see it and elevate their games. Under-confident businesses are too timid to move boldly ahead in rapidly changing times. They stay in their cozy little comfort zones as the world and their competition pass them by.

Confidence is the fuel that fires the self-fulfilling prophecy phenomenon. Our lives are just a constant series of "now" moments. Each "now" affects all future "now" moments. If you feel confident that some event will occur in the present moment, it casts a positive spell over the future "now" moments and increases the likelihood of their occurrence. The opposite is also true. So success in life or in business isn't a single event. It's a long-term success cycle that gains momentum as it repeats, as shown in the diagram below.

LONG-TERM SUCCESS CYCLE

You feel confident.

You take inspired action.

You achieve success.

Tiger has always felt confident in his abilities. His parents and Team Tiger have made sure of that. This confidence has led him to take inspired action, both in terms of his practice ethic and his actions during competition. This inspired action (coupled with his natural talent) has created success on a spectacular and regular basis. His success has made him even more confident, which leads to more inspired action, more success and more . . . well, you get the idea.

The bottom line: Tiger doesn't hope he can win. He doesn't know he can win. He expects to win. Need three statistics to back up that assertion? (1) Tiger is the greatest "closer" of all time. He has won an amazing thirty-seven out of forty tournaments when he is leading or tied for the lead entering the final round. (2) When Tiger is leading or tied for the lead after fifty-four holes in a major championship, he has won all twelve times. (3) Tiger's playoff record is an astounding fourteen wins and one loss. And remember, in playoffs Tiger is competing against golfers who played just as well as he did over the previous seventy-two holes. If you factor in that two of his playoffs had three participants, there's a one in 18,432 possibility of that happening by chance. A record of fourteen and one is no accident. It's confidence and skill in action.

Confidence—A Key Factor in Long-Term Success

Pioneer aviator Beryl Markham once said, "Success breeds confidence." I would add, "Confidence that leads to inspired action eventually leads to success." By any standard, Tiger has been successful on the golf course every year since he was two years old. Consider a sampling of his accomplishments through the years.

Age 2: Appears on CBS News and the *Mike Douglas Show,* playing golf with Bob Hope.

Age 3: Shoots a score of 48 for nine holes.

Age 5: Appears on the TV show *That's Incredible.*

Ages 6–15: Wins Optimist International Junior World Tournaments at ages eight, nine, twelve, thirteen, fourteen, and fifteen. Is the youngest ever to win the U.S. Junior Amateur Championship.

Ages 16 & 17: Wins the U.S. Junior Amateur Championship two more times. Is the only person to win more than once.

Ages 18–20: Wins three U.S. Amateur Championships in a row. Is the only person to accomplish this. Turns professional and wins two tournaments.

Age 21: Wins the Masters tournament and is leading money winner on the professional tour.

Age 22: Wins almost $3 million and three tournaments worldwide.

Age 23: Wins PGA Championship and ten other tournaments worldwide.

Age 24: Lowest per-round scoring average for an entire year in the history of professional golf—68.17 strokes per round. Wins over $9 million on the PGA Tour (the most ever) and over $11 million worldwide (the most ever). Wins three major tournaments and six others on the PGA Tour.

Age 25: Wins Masters Tournament to become the only person ever to be the reigning champion in all four major tournaments.

Age 26: Leading money winner on the PGA Tour for the fourth consecutive year. Wins Masters Tournament and U.S. Open championship.

Age 27: Breaks an all-time record when he extends his streak of 114 consecutive events without missing a cut.* Wins $7.4 million worldwide.

Age 28: Sets the record with 264 consecutive weeks as the world's top-ranked golfer. (The previous record was 96 weeks.) Becomes the top career money winner on the PGA Tour with $45 million.

Age 29: Wins the Masters Tournament and the British Open.

Age 30: Wins six PGA tournaments in a row, including two of the majors—the British Open and the PGA Championship.

In case you weren't counting, that's twenty-eight years of continuous success. That's a trend!

The CREAM Approach to Creating Confidence in Your Business Team

Just as the people in Team Tiger created confidence in Tiger, you can create confidence in your organization with the CREAM approach:

- Celebrate team victories.
- Recognize and reward individual and team behavior.

---

*In most tournaments, golfers play thirty-six holes. Then the players with the lowest scores go on to play another thirty-six holes. If players don't shoot low enough, they "miss the cut."

- Encourage and expect inspired action.
- Articulate dreams and goals.
- Model desired behavior.

To be chronologically correct, let's start at the end of the acronym and work backward.

Model Desired Behavior

Earl and Tida modeled the attitudes, beliefs, and behaviors they wanted to see in their son. They understood the power of personal example. You need to do the same with the people in your organization: Demonstrate the behaviors and attitudes you want your team to adopt. Your deeds have way more power than your words.

Articulate Dreams and Goals

As you've learned in previous chapters, Tiger's dream and the goals that will be accomplished on the path to its achievement are crystal clear. Follow his example by clearly and consistently articulating your organization's dream as well as its short- and long-term goals—and your confidence that they will be achieved.

Encourage and Expect Inspired Action

In the last Tiger Trait, you learned how Team Tiger consistently provided the encouragement "fertilizer" that allowed Tiger's natural talent to blossom. I also suspect that Earl and Tida believed that Tiger's sensational successes on the golf course and in life were somehow preordained. They expected their son to accomplish great things. Do the same with your group. Encourage them. Believe in them. Expect them to do the right things. In other words, treat them like the people you know they will become.

Recognize and Reward Individual and Team Behavior

Tiger receives the confidence boost of being recognized as the best golfer in the world today. He receives financial rewards in the neighborhood of $100 million a year. I realize that you can't do the same with the people in your organization, but I'll bet you can do a better job of recognizing and rewarding. How many times a day do you praise, compliment, or thank your team members? How often do you publicly recognize and reward outstanding contributions by groups and individuals? If you're doing it only twelve times a year with an Employee of the Month award, maybe you need to increase the frequency and variety.

I know you care about the people you work with. The $64,000 question is, do they know it? Tiger has received the coveted green jacket for each one of his Masters victories. Do you have a plethora of meaningful "green jacket" rewards for the people in your organization? If not, get started now.

> *Do you single out individuals for public praise and recognition? Do you make people who work for you feel important? If you honor and serve them, they will honor and serve you.*
> —Mary Kay Ash

Celebrate Team Victories

Tiger celebrated his victory at the 1997 Masters with his team that night. Do you celebrate your team's victories in similar fashion? If there aren't enough victories right now in your organization, maybe you should follow Rudy Duran's lead by

creating achievable "Tiger pars" and celebrating their achievement. That will jump-start your group's Long-Term Success
Cycle. They will experience success and feel the confidence
needed to take their next inspired actions.

Practicing CREAM will enable your team to rise to the top.
They will now have complete confidence in the form of confidence in themselves, confidence in their teammates, confidence in leadership, confidence in their company's business
model and strategic plan, and confidence in the achievement
of the organization's goals and vision.

As an added bonus, outsiders will have confidence in you,
too, and want to invest in your organization, come to work
with you, partner with you, and buy your products or services.
Complete confidence is magical. It energizes and improves
everything it comes in contact with. Allow its magic to be a
primary goal of your organization.

Passing the Confidence Torch

For the first two rounds of the 2000 PGA Championship, Tiger
was paired with Jack Nicklaus for the first time in tournament play. Tiger was playing extremely well. Jack was playing
well for a man of his age, but it was obvious that he would not
make the cut and be allowed to play the final two rounds of
the tournament. As the two legends were walking off the eighteenth tee, Tiger told Jack, "It's been an honor and a privilege
to play with you. Let's finish off on the correct note."

Jack replied, "You got it. Let's go." Jack and Tiger both
made birdies on the final hole. The confidence torch officially
had been passed.

Your Next Tiger Trait

When sprinkled on natural talent, confidence is the magic elixir that allows the talent to blossom into extraordinary performance. Another inner attribute that does the same is to find and adopt magnificent mental models. I'm confident that you will read on to discover how to manufacture them.

TIGER TRAIT# ⑤

MANUFACTURE MAGNIFICENT MENTAL MODELS

Life does not consist mainly of facts and happenings.
It consists mainly of the storm of thoughts
that is forever blowing through one's head.

—Mark Twain

MARK TWAIN WAS RIGHT: Most of what we see is not "out there." Most of what we see is produced in our own minds. In truth, we typically use only small amounts of the information we receive from the outside world. Instead, we discard most of it and focus only on a very few bits of input at one time. As Jerry Wind and Colin Crook state in their must-read book, *The Power of Impossible Thinking*, "The real world does exist. We just ignore most of it."

Do you need evidence that you ignore most of the real world? Without looking at the face of your wristwatch, imagine an accurate and complete representation of it. Now look at your watch. How did you do? If you're like most people, you left out key features and/or you mentally added features that shouldn't be there. How can this be? You look at your watch dozens of times a day. It's because you look at the watch hands and ignore the rest.

Here's another example of your "ignore"-ance. Read the following paragraph.

> Aoccdrnig to rseearch at an Elingsh uinervtisy, it deons't mttaer in waht oredr the ltteers in a wrod are, olny taht the frist and lsat ltteres are in the rghit pcleas. The rset can be a toatl mses and you can sitll raed it wouthit a porbelm. Tihs is bcuseae we do not raed ervey lteter by ilstef, but the wrod as a wlohe.

This scrambled paragraph is a perfect demonstration of how the brain works to create meaning from even the most messed-up circumstances by focusing on some information and ignoring the rest. Do you ignore as much information in the rest of your life? The answer is yes. We're constantly ignoring parts of the world because our brains have categorized the information as nonessential. But sometimes not seeing this "nonessential" information can trip us up. How many times have you looked at a business plan or memo from a colleague and thought it was fine, only to have someone with a fresh perspective point out a problem you missed? Even more challenging, are there character traits or aspects of your personality that you don't notice but which have gotten in your way when it comes to a promotion, or being considered for a big project, or kept you from getting the performance review you believe you deserved?

To make sense of our world, we need to learn what to pay attention to and what to ignore. When Tiger lines up a putt, he knows exactly what's going to be important to his shot—the condition of the green, the distance from the hole, whether the green breaks left or right, and so on. He also knows that it's probably safe to ignore a lot of extraneous information, such as the people in the gallery, background noise, or where the other golfers are standing, for example. In business, we must learn again and again what's important in any situation, so we can pay attention to the small things that will have the biggest impact. We must pay attention to the 20 percent of the factors that will make 80 percent of the difference.

Mental Models in Action

Wind and Crook use the term *mental models* to describe the brain processes that help us make sense of our world. Mental models are constructed in our three-pound brains using our 100 billion neurons (nerve cells) and one quadrillion synapses (connections between neurons). Our mental models act like the director of a movie: They decide which scenes are included and excluded in the movie; where the camera is pointed in each scene; whether the camera shot is a close-up, a wide-angle, or a panorama, and so on. They also have the ability to distort the footage shot with "special effects." In the end, our mental models construct "virtual reality" simulations (mind movies) of our world. We then act on these simulations, not external reality.

Mental models affect every aspect of our personal and professional lives, as well as our society as a whole. Here are some examples.

Personal

Have you ever been in a situation with two other people, and an external event occurs that affects all of you? For instance, you and two colleagues have flown in for a big meeting with a new client. While you're in the reception area, someone comes in and tells you that there's been an emergency and your meeting has to be postponed until late in the day. You're all going to have to rebook your flights home. Person A gets extremely upset. You're Person B, and you ask Person A, "What are you so upset about? This is no big deal." Meanwhile Person C is over in the corner laughing like crazy. He thinks the whole situation is comical. How can one event create three completely different reactions? Three different mental models in three different brains have produced three different mind movies and the actions that automatically followed from them.

Professional

Remember the conversation between Tiger and Curtis Strange in the last chapter? The external reality was the same: a twenty-year-old man playing in his first professional tournament. The two men had strikingly diverse mental models that refracted the external reality "light beam" in two different directions. Thus, the mind movies that were projected on the screen in each man's brain were radically different. Curtis's mind movie was entitled *Do Your Best and Pay Your Dues, Young Man.* Tiger's was *I'm Here to Win This Sucker!* The conversation that followed the disparate mental movies was painfully awkward, as if the two men lived in different worlds. In truth, they did—two different inner worlds.

> *I'm about five inches from becoming an outstanding golfer. That's the distance my left ear is from my right ear.*
> —Ben Crenshaw

Societal

The O. J. Simpson trial was a graphic example of mental models at play in our society. Why did 80 percent of African Americans think O. J. was innocent and 80 percent of Caucasians think he was guilty, even though both groups watched the same external reality (trial) on TV? The two groups have vastly different mental models concerning the criminal justice system in America. These mental models created two different mind movies, which automatically led to two different versions of the truth.

How Mental Models Are Created

Here's what Wind and Crook say about mental model creation: "Our own brains change and evolve over time, with neurons constantly dying and being re-created, synapses being destroyed and created anew. The brain selects and reinforces or weakens certain synapses to forge the complex neural structures that determine our thinking. Then, we reshape these neural 'models' through experience, education, and training."

Let's look at the forces that shape and reshape your mental models, using Tiger's life as an example.

1. **Education and training**—Your formal and informal education and training—whether it's at school, in your home, on the job or as part of a religious group—will affect your mental models. Tiger's heroes and supporters have played a huge role in creating his mental models. From the very beginning, Earl and Tida dedicated themselves to educating Tiger on what to do in the world (activities) and how to view the world (mental models). Throughout this book you have and will discover how they raised Tiger to be an outstanding golfer and an even better person.

   The proof is in the pudding. Tiger's mental models work for him. If you have a mental model that isn't working for you, maybe you need to learn a new one that will help you view the world more effectively. As an example, if your English language mental model doesn't allow you to comprehend the Spanish language used by important clients in Mexico City, maybe you should add an additional mental model to your collection by taking a Spanish language course.

When I present my *Thriving on Change* program to corporate and association audiences, I primarily help them shift their mental models concerning change from "change equals pain" to "change equals opportunity." I do this because I know that mental model transformation must occur before any constructive behavior can begin. If you're a business leader, I've got a question for you. "How much time and financial resources do you spend on mental model training for your people?"

2. **Rewards and incentives**—It's estimated that Tiger earns nearly $100 million a year in prize money and endorsements. That's an incredible incentive to play a game he loves anyway! But more important than having the money is fulfilling his dream to be recognized as the greatest golfer of all time and to use his fame and resources to make the world a better place.

It's vital that you identify the rewards and incentives that work best for you. Then, whenever possible, put yourself in situations where you will receive them. Likewise, it's vital that you know the rewards and incentives work best for the people you lead. Now, you can give the proper rewards and incentives to them. Remember, money isn't the only or most important reward and incentive for many people.

3. **Personal experience**—From appearing on the *Mike Douglas Show* at age two, to his record-setting wins at the U.S. Amateur Championship, to his first Masters win in 1997 and his twelfth major champion in 2006, Tiger's life has been a cornucopia of empowering personal experiences which have enhanced his mental models.

What experiences would do the best job of enhancing your mental models? Maybe it's donating your time at a homeless shelter, going sky-diving or taking a long walk in the woods each week?

What experiences can you create for the people you lead at work that will enhance their mental models? Maybe it's having everyone participate in a ropes course or visiting a Ritz Carlton to experience their level of service.

How about your kids? Do you immerse them in character-building experiences on a regular basis?

Four Powerful Mental Models Used by Tiger

Over the years I've read and viewed over twenty books and DVDs by and about Tiger. From this mountain of information, I've discovered that he extensively uses four mental models. These models are very useful for all of us when we approach the great game of life.

1. Focus on what you want.

The one-hundredth British Open in 2000 was held at the birthplace of golf, the Old Course at St. Andrews, Scotland. Tiger won the tournament by eight strokes with a record score of 269. Impressive as that was, it was even more impressive that he missed the course's 112 strategically placed bunkers (sand traps) for four straight days. That's a total of 448 bunkers in a row! How did Tiger do it? He focused on what he wanted (his ball stopping on grass) not on what he didn't want (his ball stopping on sand).

There is way too much information in your world to focus on everything. It physically can't be done. Your mental models can come to the rescue by directing your focus. You would think that everyone would focus only on what they want, but that doesn't happen in reality. As an example, imagine that you were given $1 million to go on a shopping spree. You go to a clothing store, buy a rack of clothes you absolutely hate and bring them home. Then you visit to a furniture store, purchase ten rooms full of furniture you despise and have it all sent to your house. Next, you drop by a department store and pick out a pile of stuff you detest and have it delivered the next day. Finally, you walk into a fancy jewelry store, select a collection of the worst looking junk you see and pack that in the car. The next day, after everything has arrived, you're sitting in the middle of the merchandise you don't want and you ask yourself, "Why did I buy this stuff?" The answer is, "Because you're crazy!"

It's just as crazy to focus on things you don't want in your life. When you do that, you bring them into your brain mentally. And mental creation always precedes physical creation.

> *When we focus on abundance, our lives feel abundant.*
> *When we focus on lack, our lives feel lacking.*
> —Susan Jeffers

Tiger was trained by his dad at an early age to use Mental Model #1 when he putted. Here's how Earl describes it in his book, *Playing Through.*

You see, [Tiger] doesn't putt for distance. He putts to a picture and lets his natural athletic instincts take over. . . . I taught Tiger this method before he could barely talk. I told Tiger, "All you have to do is take your set-up stance, aim your putter, take a look at the hole and look at the ball. And look at the hole, which is the picture, and look at the ball. You will see that picture in your mind. Now roll the ball to the picture."

In your personal and professional life, do you have a picture to "roll your ball" to? If you're in a leadership position at work, do you have a picture for your people to roll the company "ball" to? Help your team focus on what everybody wants by creating and effectively communicating your company's vision. Then follow the first rule of management: Reward the actions you want to see more of.

2. Be a time traveler.

We're all time travelers: We have the ability to use our imagination to go back to our past, focus on what's happening in the moment, or travel into the future.

The Present

Most of the time, it's best to focus on the present. When you're driving to work, focus on the things happening around you in to moment. When you're at work, focus on the business at hand. When you're with your kids, be with your kids. Do you have friends who are constantly living in the past? They're always talking about the "good old days," or bringing up some terrible tragedy that warped their lives forever when they were ten years old? Didn't you feel like pulling them into the present by saying, "I know you liked the old days or you had some bad stuff happen in the past, but what are you doing *right now* to make your life better?"

The Past

So how *do* you use the past? One way is to learn from the past, both the good times and bad. Another way is to go back to the past to make yourself feel empowered in the present. You learned about Tiger doing this in Tiger Trait #4, where he and two of his friends went to see the movie *Tin Cup* one evening during the U.S. Amateur Championship. On the way back to the hotel, they stopped at a sand trap where Tiger had executed one of the most dramatic shots of his career a few years earlier. Tiger utilized the memory of that amazing shot to give him greater confidence in preparation for the next day's play.

Entering his final round of the 2006 Deutsche Bank Championship, Tiger trailed Vijay Singh by three shots. As reported in *USA Today*, while Tiger warmed up, he remembered a tournament he played in the week before, when he defeated Stewart Cink in a playoff. Tiger said to himself, "Hey, I just got it done. The circumstances are similar [to last week]. There's no reason I can't get it done now."

You, too, can use the memories of your moments of success to help you find the confidence necessary to strive for greater accomplishments.

The Future

If you focus on things you don't want to have happen in the future, you feel bad in the present and you leave yourself open to a negative self-fulfilling prophecy where you create what you don't want. The reverse is also true. When you focus on what you do want to happen in the future, you can feel good in the present and tap the power of a positive self-fulfilling prophecy. That's why Tiger Trait #2, "Create a Clear and Compelling Dream," is so important. It automatically focuses you in the direction of your dreams.

Before Tiger hits each shot, he travels through time. As he walks up to the ball, he may recall a well-played shot previously played from a similar position or under a similar pressure situation in the *past*. Then, right before he hits the shot, he may imagine a detailed movie clip of the *future* flight path of the ball, seeing it landing and coming to rest. Then he imagines the swing that will produce the shot. Finally, he shifts to the *present* and allows his training to take over as he executes the perfect swing. I've seen Tiger playing in tournaments. On the course he is all business, because time traveling takes concentration. That's why Tiger has said, "I don't talk much to my fellow players because I'm too busy concentrating, in my own world taking care of business."

3. Zoom in, zoom out.

When you zoom in, you focus more intently on the details of the situation. When you zoom out, you see the big picture. Both are important in your personal life and in business. In your personal life, it's a great idea to sit down at the beginning of the week and zoom out on all your family and personal desires for the entire week. Then, during the week, zoom in as you take action on the individual desires. As an example, be totally zoomed in on your daughter as you help with her homework.

In business, you might zoom in on the execution of a specific initiative of your company, then zoom out as you examine how that initiative may affect the other aspects of your business. Smart "mice" zoom in on the "cheese" directly in front of them. They also zoom out to see if the cheese is sitting in a mousetrap. You should do the same.

Zooming out and zooming in are the keys to navigating complex information. It's the antidote for being too nearsighted or too farsighted. The game of golf is the perfect example. Before Tiger hits a 180-yard shot into a green, he zooms out and examines the context of the situation:

- His need to hit a precise shot or a safe shot
- The accuracy with which he has been hitting similar shots that day
- The distance to the pin
- Where the pin is positioned on the green
- The varying slopes of the green
- The speed of the green
- The hazards around the green
- The speed, direction, and variability of the wind
- The change in elevation from his ball to the pin
- How his ball is sitting in the grass
- Whether the ball is equal to, above, or below his feet

Then and only then does he zoom in on the swing he needs to hit the shot he desires.

Whether you zoom in or zoom out first depends on the situation. If you're in a short-term crisis situation, zoom in on solving the crisis first. Then zoom out on why the crisis occurred in the first place and how you can prevent it from happening again. For a negative situation that isn't a crisis, zoom out on the causes of the situation and the resources available. Then zoom in on the actions you need to take to resolve the situation. If you are overwhelmed by everything you have to do in a day, zoom out by creating a to-do list of specific actions you will do and the order in which you will accomplish them. Then zoom in on doing the first action.

In Viktor Frankl's superb book, *Man's Search for Meaning*, he wrote the following passage about zooming out under extremely trying circumstances.

> We who lived in the concentration camps can remember the men who walked through the huts comforting others, giving away their last piece of bread. They may have been few in number, but they offer sufficient proof that everything can be taken from a man but one thing: the last of human freedom—to choose one's attitude in any given set of circumstances.

4. Bounce back.

For most of his professional career, Tiger has been at or near the top of a statistical category called "bounce back," which is a measure of how likely players are to make birdies or better on the hole after they make bogeys or worse. Tiger bounces back about one-third of the time. If he hits a poor shot, he's learned to "hit it and forget it." When Tiger hits a bad shot, he learns a lesson from the mistake, and then moves on to the next shot without the negative baggage of the last shot. That's a great lesson for all of us.

Conclusion

Our mental models are so powerful, invisible, and persistent that when the old models no longer explain what is happening in our worlds, we keep trying to make our current experiences fit into them. Apple's Steve Jobs has turned the music industry upside down with his iPod digital devices and iTunes music purchasing system. Why didn't the big players in the music industry beat him to the punch? Their powerful, invisible, and persistent mental models blinded them from innovative

thinking. With his mental models, Steve created a vastly different means of delivering music to the world.

> *One's destination is never a place,*
> *but rather a new way of looking at things.*
>   —Henry Miller

Your Next Tiger Trait

You're over halfway through your "round." In Tiger Trait #1,
you learned how to identify and develop your natural talents.
In Trait #2, you learned why creating a clear and compelling dream that utilizes your natural talents is vital to success
and happiness. In Trait #3, you learned why it's necessary to
select the right collection of teachers, heroes, and teammates
to guide, inspire, and support the attainment of your dream.
In Trait #4, you learned why developing a high level of confidence is mandatory to harness the power of your talents,
dreams, and knowledge. In Trait #5, you learned why magnificent mental models are needed to create the mental movies
you need to navigate your complex world. In the next Tiger
Trait, you will explore the power of letting actions do the talking. Take some action now by flipping the page.

TIGER TRAIT# 6

LET ACTIONS DO THE TALKING

IN TIGER TRAIT #3, you discovered how Tiger won his first major tournament, the 1997 Masters, in record-setting fashion. Expectations were sky-high for the future of young Mr. Woods. However, for reasons you will discover later, he didn't win a major tournament in his next ten attempts—a period of over two years. Some people began to doubt Tiger's ability to achieve his dream of being the greatest golfer of all time. Tiger didn't say much to the naysayers about his so-called slump. Instead, he followed his mother's advice, "Let your clubs speak for you."

After winning the 1999 PGA championship, his clubs regained their voice in June of 2000, at the one-hundredth U.S. Open at Pebble Beach, California. In addition to being the centennial event, it was Jack Nicklaus' farewell U.S. Open. Tiger's clubs began to speak in the opening round when he shot a sixty-five for a three-stroke lead. His clubs talked even louder during his second round of sixty-nine, which expanded his lead to six. In the horrible weather of the third round, his clubs were shouting, as his score of seventy-one increased his lead to ten shots. They were screaming at the top of their lungs as he posted a score of sixty-seven on the final round. Tiger's fifteen-stoke victory margin was four better than the previous record. In the history of the U.S. Open, nobody has ever shot lower in relation to par.

The win at Pebble Beach was the beginning of the greatest year ever in golf history. Tiger went on to win the remaining two majors that year—the British Open and the PGA Championship—and seven other PGA tournaments. His worldwide winnings of over $11 million were another record. Tiger went on to win the first major of 2001, the Masters, to become the first person to have all four major trophies on his mantel at the same time. To say the least, his clubs had spoken eloquently and emphatically for an entire year.

Tida's Sage Advice

Because of Tiger's race (his father is half African American, a quarter American Indian and a quarter Chinese, and his mother is half Thai, a quarter Chinese and a quarter white), as a child Tiger experienced racism on numerous occasions on and off the golf course. Each time this happened, his mother would say, "When you've been wronged, when you've been angered, you need not say anything. *Let your clubs speak for you.*"

Tida knew that two wrongs don't make a right. She knew that if Tiger responded hostilely to the injustices directed toward him, his actions would be controlled by the attacker. By letting his clubs speak for him, Tiger could demonstrate that he was in control of his emotions and actions—that *he* was choosing to take The Hero's Journey.

The Hero's Journey

In many ways, the story of Tiger Woods follows the storyline of a classical myth—the hero's journey. Countless movies and novels are based upon this momentous myth. In it, the hero leaves his comfortable, ordinary surroundings to venture into a challenging, unfamiliar world. The journey is usually an external one to an actual place—a labyrinth, a forest, a cave, a strange land, a new neighborhood or city. The new location becomes the arena for his conflict with antagonistic and challenging forces.

But the hero's story is also an internal journey of the mind, heart and spirit. The hero grows and changes, making the journey from one way of life to the next—from ignorance to wisdom, from hate to love, or from weakness to strength.

In Christopher Vogler's fascinating book *The Writer's Journey: Mythic Structure for Storytellers and Screenwriters* he arranges the hero's journey into three acts and twelve scenes.

Act One—The Hero's Decision to Make the Journey

The Ordinary World—The ordinary world creates a vivid contrast to the strange new world the hero is about to enter. For example, in *Star Wars,* Luke Skywalker was an average teenager growing up on his aunt and uncle's farm. Tiger Woods was the son of seemingly ordinary parents living in a modest, suburban neighborhood.

Call to Adventure—The hero is presented with a problem, challenge, or adventure to undertake. The hero is no longer comfortable in the ordinary world. The call to adventure establishes the stakes of the game and clarifies the hero's goal—to win the treasure, capture the heart of the loved one, right a wrong, confront a challenge, or achieve a dream. In Star Wars, Obi-Wan Kenobi asks Luke to rescue Princess Leia from Darth Vader. Tiger feels the call to excel in golf.

Refusal of the Call—The hero hesitates at the threshold of the adventure because of his fear of the unknown. Often a second influence is needed to spur the hero on the journey— another offense against the natural order of things, or the encouragement of a mentor. Luke refuses the call and returns to the farm, only to find that the storm troopers have barbecued his aunt and uncle. Now, he's motivated. Tiger is unusual in that he never refused the call. Most of us do.

Meeting with the Mentor—The mentor is often a wise old man or woman. The relationship between the hero and mentor stands for the bond between parent and child, teacher and student, or God and humanity. However, the mentor can take the hero only so far: eventually, the hero will have to go it alone. Luke had Obi-Wan Kenobi and Han Solo as mentors. Tiger's parents were his early mentors.

Crossing the First Threshold—The hero commits to the adventure and fully enters a special world for the first time. He agrees to face the challenge posed in the call to adventure. There is no turning back. In *Star Wars,* Luke begins his voyage to face Darth Vader. Tiger begins playing in junior golf tournaments.

Act Two—The Journey

Tests, Allies, and Enemies—Once across the first threshold, the hero encounters new challenges and tests, makes allies and enemies, and starts to learn the rules of the new world. Luke meets Han Solo, goes to the Alien Bar and learns a few lessons from his mentors. Tiger faces early golf matches with older and bigger boys. He forms alliances with Rudy Duran, Jay Brunza, and John Anselmo. Tiger faces discrimination and resistance from people who are uncomfortable with his ethnicity and phenomenal skill.

Approach to the Inmost Cave—The inmost cave is the most dangerous place in the new world. The hero often pauses at the gate to prepare, plan, and outwit the villain's guards. In *Star Wars,* Luke approaches the Death Star and the evil Lord Vader. In *The Wizard of Oz,* Dorothy approaches the city of Oz and its mysterious wizard. Sometimes the inmost cave is inhabited by a truly formidable force (Darth). Sometimes it's inhabited by a force the hero only *thinks* is formidable (the wizard). Tiger approaches his inmost cave when he begins to compete as a professional on the PGA Tour in August of 1996.

The Supreme Ordeal—The fortunes of the hero hit bottom in a direct confrontation with his greatest fear. The hero faces the possibility of death in a battle with a hostile force. Luke's spaceship is sucked into the Death Star, where he comes face to face with his greatest fear. In 1996, Tiger needs to earn $125,000 in the seven PGA events in which he is playing to earn his PGA Tour membership card for the following year. After five events, he still hasn't done it.

Reward—After the hero survives the supreme ordeal, he celebrates and receives the treasure, magic sword, or elixir that can heal the wounded land. He may also receive better understanding of another person or group of people. Luke defeats Darth Vader and rescues Princess Leia. The Federation is safe, for now at least. In 1996, Tiger wins his sixth tournament, which qualifies him for the PGA Tour in 1997. He puts icing on the cake as he wins the Masters in 1997.

Act Three—The Consequences of the Journey

The Road Back—The hero is not out of the woods yet. The evil forces will chase him home, trying to recover their lost reward. The road back marks the decision to return to the ordinary world. The hero realizes that the special world must be left behind. There are still dangers, temptations, and tests ahead. Luke escapes the Death Star with Leia as Darth follows in hot pursuit. Tiger doesn't win another major tournament for over two years. Many people begin to doubt him.

Resurrection—This is the hero's final exam, to make sure he has learned the lessons of the supreme ordeal. It is often a second life-or-death encounter with the forces of evil. Luke faces and defeats Darth Vader again. Beginning with the 2000 U.S. Open, Tiger wins four consecutive major tournaments—a feat never before accomplished.

Return with Elixir—The hero returns to the ordinary world, but the journey is meaningless unless he brings back some elixir, treasure, or lesson from the special world. In *The Wizard of Oz,* Dorothy now knows that "There's no place like home!" Unless something of value is brought back from the journey to the inmost cave, the hero is doomed to repeat the adventure. In the movie *Groundhog Day,* the Bill Murray character had to repeat the same day over and over until he learned the required lesson. Luke returns to his ordinary world knowing that he has the skills of the Jedi. Tiger knows that he was destined to be a major positive force on the golf course in particular and the world in general.

The wonderful American author Willa Cather wrote, "There are only two or three human stories, and they go on repeating themselves as fiercely as if they had never happened before." One of those human stories is the hero's journey.

Luke Skywalker's journey in *Star Wars* is universally popular because it taps into a powerful drive within all of us—the drive to be a hero. I believe Tiger Woods is universally popular with people of all ages and demographics for the same reason. His life magically resonates with our desire to be heroes.

Here are some hero's journey questions for you to consider.

1. At what stage are you on the hero's journey?

2. Have you ever refused the call to adventure? When? Why? What eventually prodded you to accept the call?

3. Who are your mentors? What additional mentors will you need?

4. What tests have you faced? What tests lie ahead?

5. What was or will be your inmost cave? What did or will allow you to win the battle?

6. What reward do you seek on your hero's journey?

7. What "final exams" did or will you face in your resurrection?

8. What internal and external elixirs will you bring back from your journey?

Enthusiastically and Intelligently Take Action

Albert Einstein sagely remarked, "Nothing happens until something moves." People on the hero's journey know that "something" is they themselves. While others are on the park benches of life watching it all go by, heroes are enthusiastically and intelligently marching down the paths to their dreams.

Watch Tiger when he sinks a long putt, or when he knows he's won a tournament: He pumps his fist in the air, and the enthusiasm that has been bottled up inside him finally explodes to the surface. Some golf "purists" frown on such behavior on the golf course, but the general public loves it. They love to see heroes displaying enthusiasm in the quest for their dreams.

Enthusiasm is magical. It transforms resolutions into realities. The word *enthusiasm* is derived from the Greek root *en Theos,* meaning "the God within." That's a hint as to its origin and its power.

> *Enthusiasm is at the bottom of all progress.*
> *With it there is accomplishment.*
> *Without it there are only alibis.*
> —Henry Ford

How does Tiger create the emotion of enthusiasm? With his mind and body. He focuses on his short-term goal of winning each tournament he enters and on his long-term goal of being the greatest golfer ever and making a major, positive contribution to society. He also "does" enthusiasm with his body. As you remember from Trait #4, he moves in confident ways to create confidence, and he also moves in enthusiastic ways to create enthusiasm.

> *I don't sing because I'm happy.*
> *I'm happy because I sing.*
> —William James

Enthusiasm is not enough, however. People who are just excited but don't know what they're doing are dangerous.

Don't be dangerous: In addition to being enthusiastic, be intelligent on your hero's journey. Tiger does all of the following. You should, too.

- Start your journey from where you are right now. Don't wait for something external to happen before you begin. You might be waiting forever. There is rarely a perfect time to begin.

> *I never worry about action, but only about inaction.*
> —Winston Churchill

- Don't recreate the wheel. Learn from other people's experience. Tiger is a first-rate example of this.
- Like Tiger, create a "Team You"—a group of teachers, heroes, and teammates to guide, inspire, and support you on your journey.
- Create and follow an intelligent action plan to get you from where you are now to where you want to go.
- Take great care of yourself. If you "blow a tire," your journey will come to a screeching halt.
- On your journey, remember what's really important in life. Take great care of the people you love along the way.

Facing the Challenges of the Hero's Journey

The paths that all heroes take on their journeys contain challenges. In fact, challenges are life's way of letting heroes know they're making progress. Tiger has faced a multitude of challenges in his young life, and he has moved through or jumped over all of them. Each time he did, he moved on to a new set of challenges that enabled him to grow to the next level.

> *If you find a path with no obstacles,*
> *it probably doesn't lead anywhere.*
> —Frank Clark

The flight of the eagle is a fitting example for the value of challenges in our lives. An eagle can fly at about thirty-five miles an hour. The air resistance in its face holds it back from flying faster. How fast do you think the eagle could fly if all the air resistance were removed? It couldn't fly at all—it would fall to the ground. No air resistance means an absence of air. If there were no air, the eagle's wings would have nothing to push against as they flap. If there were no air, nothing would flow over the eagle's wings to create lift. In other words, the resistance the eagle faces is also a necessity for flight. It's the same in life. Life's challenges are a necessity for growth.

> *If you can meet with triumph and disaster and treat these*
> *two imposters just the same . . . you'll be a man, my son!*
> —Rudyard Kipling

Earl knew that Tiger would face challenges when he was on the course. That's why Earl created the "Woods' Finishing School" when Tiger was twelve. In training Tiger, Earl did everything he could to distract his son on the course. He'd cough or drop clubs during his swing, toss a ball in front of him just as Tiger was getting ready to shoot, tell him, "Don't hit your ball into the water," and so on. Tiger wasn't permitted to say a word about his dad's tactics. Earl's goal was to prepare his son for the rigors of professional golf. The Woods' Finishing School helped make Tiger mentally tough at an early age.

Enjoy the Journey

Tiger's parents never forced him to practice golf. They knew that for him to be successful in any endeavor in life, he must enjoy the journey. People receive their enjoyment in individual ways. Earl once asked Tiger why he didn't relax and enjoy the beauty of the golf course. Tiger answered that he enjoyed himself by shooting low scores.

> *There are two things to aim at in life:*
> *First to get what you want; And after that, to enjoy it.*
> *Only the wisest of mankind achieve the second.*
> —Logan Pearsall Smith

One of Tiger's heroes is golf legend Arnold Palmer. When Palmer was asked for the secret to his success, he replied, "Hit the ball hard. Go find it. Hit it again." I have a feeling that he was referring to the game of golf and the game of life. His comments above could be restated as, "Take massive action. Evaluate the results of your massive action. Then, take some more action."

Your Next Tiger Trait

Tiger Trait #6 was all about action, but all actions can be improved. Constantly improving in good times and bad is the subject of the next Tiger Trait. Read on. You will be better for it.

TIGER TRAIT#7

CONSTANTLY IMPROVE IN GOOD TIMES AND BAD

IN TIGER TRAIT #3, "Select Teachers, Heroes, and Teammates Who Guide, Inspire, and Support," you learned about Tiger's first major victory at the 1997 Masters, where he won by posting the lowest score ever. He had just beaten the world's best golfers by twelve strokes. Tiger was at the top of golf's totem pole. But he also had a golf swing that wasn't consistent. So, after the biggest win of his career, he decided to completely retool his swing—no small task, as any golfer will tell you. Tiger told his swing coach, Butch Harmon, "I want to change it now!" Tiger knew that, even in the very best of times, he needed to improve his swing to keep the dream alive.

Tiger went two years and played in ten majors before he would win his second one. But that was just the lull before the storm. In 1999, at the age of twenty-three, Tiger won ten PGA tournaments, including the PGA Championship. In 2000, he got even better. He won twelve tournaments around the world, including the U.S. Open Championship, the British Open Championship, and the PGA Championship. The day after he won the 2000 PGA Championship, at a time when Tiger was the toast of the town, he was on the practice range near his home, improving his skills. With his win at the Masters in 2001, he became the first person to be reigning champion in all four at one time.

> *I never met any athlete who worked*
> *as hard on his game as Tiger.*
>   —Charles Barkley

Learning from Disappointment

It hasn't been a straight shot to success for Tiger Woods. Like all daring dreamers, he encountered disappointments along the way. But like all the travelers on the hero's journey, Tiger learned something from each of them.

- In the Los Angeles Open, his first tournament as a sixteen-year-old amateur playing against a field of professionals, Tiger was five over par for the first two rounds and missed the cut by six strokes. Tiger's response was, "I'm very disappointed I didn't make the cut. But give me some time to grow up, and I'll be back. It's still the two best days of my life."

- When he was a sophomore in high school, on the final hole of the league championship Tiger four-putted from thirty feet. (Two putts from that distance is normal.) Tiger's response? "Carelessness is costly."

- In his first attempt to qualify for the U.S. Open, Tiger missed it by four strokes. His dad's assessment was, "It's just part of the maturation process, part of the game plan."

- As an amateur, Tiger missed the cut in his next three tournaments against professionals. Tiger's response, "There's a lot I need to learn to move to the next level."

- Then, Tiger lost a local junior tournament he had won six times previously by eight strokes. Tiger's reaction, "I've lost interest at this level of golf now. I'm ready to move to the next level."

Do you notice some similarities in the five situations mentioned above? In each situation, Tiger was disappointed, and in each situation he took the negative emotion of disappointment and used it as a signal that he needed to learn a valuable lesson. Most people let disappointment hold them back. Tiger harnesses the power of disappointment to thrust him forward.

Practice, Practice, Practice

Golf is a game whose aim is to hit
a very small ball into an even smaller hole,
with weapons singularly ill designed for that purpose.
—Winston Churchill

If you play golf, you know what Churchill means. Even with tons of natural talent like Tiger has, golf is a difficult game to master. Tiger knew the secret to mastery when he was only six years old. Tiger already had made two holes-in-one. People would ask him, "How did you get so good, Tiger?" And he would answer, "Practice, practice, practice."

*What we do best or most perfectly is what we have most
thoroughly learned by the longest practice; and at length
it falls from us without our notice, as a leaf from a tree.*

—Henry David Thoreau

It's commonly recognized that, even though Tiger is dominating golf, he works the hardest at his game. Earlier in this chapter you learned about Tiger's overpowering victory in the 2000 U.S. Open. What I didn't mention was the day before the tournament Tiger spent ten hours practicing his game only to find that he wasn't satisfied with his putting stroke. So, at a time of the day when his competitors were eating dinner, Tiger went back to the practice green for two more hours to discover the problem and refine his stroke. His practice, practice, practice paid off. Over the next four days, he didn't have a three-putt in 72 holes of championship golf.

The four athletes who have transcended their sports and received global recognition from even non-sports fans for their exploits are Muhammad Ali in boxing, Michael Jordan in basketball, Pele in soccer, and Tiger Woods in golf. They all had extraordinary levels of God-given talent, and they all practiced, practiced, practiced longer and harder than their rivals. As usual, Muhammad Ali summed it up eloquently when he said, "The fight is won or lost far away from the witnesses. It is won behind the scenes, in the gym, out there on the road, long before I dance under the lights."

*Excellence is an art won by training and habituation.
We do not act rightly because we have virtue or
excellence, but we rather have those because we
have acted rightly. We are what we repeatedly do.
Excellence, then, is not an act but a habit.*

—Aristotle

Four Stages of Mastery

It's easy to take Tiger's mastery of the game of golf for granted. But becoming a virtuoso on the links is a four-stage process that we all must travel to attain mastery in any field of endeavor.

Stage One—Unconscious Incompetence

When you're unconsciously incompetent, you don't know that you don't know. There was a time very early in his life when Tiger didn't know that he didn't know about golf. In stage one, you're ignorant. There's nothing wrong with that. Ignorance is the first stage of mastery.

Stage Two—Conscious Incompetence

When you're consciously incompetent, you know that you don't know. There was a short period of time when Tiger was in his high chair, watching Earl hit balls into the net, that he knew that he didn't know how to do the same. Knowledge moves you from stage one to stage two. In stage two, you're motivated to take action.

Stage Three—Conscious Competence

At this stage, you know what to do and you can perform the activity, but you have to put all your focus on doing it. You're competent, but the activity doesn't feel natural. Tiger Woods is extremely unusual in that he didn't go through this stage when he first swung a golf club. But when he retooled his swing after the 1997 Masters, he did have to consciously think about the new activity. His results reflected the challenges he was having: Tiger didn't win another major tournament for over two years.

What moves you from stage two to stage three? A decision. You have to decide to make the commitment to learning how to perform the activity so you can become consciously competent. Then, only incessant and consistent practice will move you from stage three to stage four.

Stage Four—Unconscious Competence

When you're unconsciously competent, you can do the activity without thinking about it. It seems natural to you. This happened to Tiger in the later stages of his swing overhaul. His swing coach, Butch Harmon, had him practice the same move for thirty minutes, until Tiger felt as if his arms were going to fall off. But as a result of his patience and perseverance, the new swing became natural to him.

> *My body does the work, and I just sit back and let it happen.*
> —Tiger Woods

In stage four, you're a master—but that doesn't mean you can relax. As Tiger knows, practice is the only thing that will keep you in stage four. You must consistently keep working at your skills so your body and mind will respond appropriately without having to think. For every hour of a tournament Tiger spends days preparing, so he can be unconsciously competent when the time comes. That's the real secret of mastery—incessant, consistent practice.

A Second So-Called Slump

In 2002, Tiger won the U.S. Open—his eighth major victory. He was twenty-six years old. After that, in the off-season, Tiger experienced three significant changes in his life:

- He had knee surgery.
- He split with his long-time swing coach, Butch Harmon.
- Because his body was growing and maturing, he made further substantial changes in his swing.

In 2003, even though he had the lowest adjusted scoring average on the PGA Tour, he won "only" five PGA tournaments, and none of them were major victories. In 2004, he won "only" three times on the Tour (no majors again) and collected "only" $7.3 million in worldwide prize winnings. Just like five years before, people started to doubt Tiger. "Maybe he's burned out?" "Maybe he's injury-prone and has a body that won't hold up on the Tour?" "Maybe he's lost interest?" Maybe? Maybe? Maybe?

Tiger never doubted. Doubts are the silent assassins of dreams. Doubts are sneaky. They lurk in the dark corners of your mind and subconsciously generate excuses why your dream won't come true. Doubts corral you in a comfortable cage—away from your thoughts of a better tomorrow. Tiger never doubted. All he did was improve. He said, "Failure does not shape your personality. It's how you react to the failure." If failure causes you to work to get stronger, then you will succeed in the end.

The Three Stages of Change

Any time you make a change—whether it's improving your golf swing, moving your family from one city to another or leading a new initiative in your company—you will go through three stages of change. To maximize your chances of success, it's vital that you understand and enthusiastically and intelligently move through the stages.

Stage One—Letting Go of the Old

As strange as it might seem, the first stage of all change is an ending. Let's use the trapeze as a metaphor. Trapeze artists fly through the air with the greatest of ease, but before they do that, they swing on bar #1 high above the ground. For them to make a change, they must let go of the bar. This can be difficult in the circus tent or in real life. You feel comfortable on bar #1. You fear the potential negative consequences if you take the leap and let go.

When Tiger made the changes to his swing in 1997 and 2002, he had to leave his old swing behind. For most people this would be a difficult choice, because Tiger had been wildly successful with that swing. However, he knew the swing that got him to where he was would not get him to where he wanted to go. So he made the leap of faith.

> *One doesn't discover new lands without consenting to lose sight of the shore for a very long time.*
> —André Gide

Stage Two—Transitioning Between the Old and the New

Stage two is the limbo period between the old and the new. Now, you're flying through the air, but usually with the greatest of unease. You may long for the good old days and constantly be looking back to bar #1. Or you may be staring down at the ground because you're afraid of what's going to happen if your flight isn't successful. Either way, your chances of catching bar #2 are zero. Even if you're doing somersaults in mid-air, you need to scope out bar #2 every once in a while.

In other words, you must keep your eyes on a successful outcome, not on painful potential failures.

> *It's not so much that we're afraid to change or so in love with the old ways, but it's that place in between that we fear. It's like being between two trapezes. It's Linus with his blanket in the dryer. There is nothing to hold on to.*
> —Marilyn Ferguson

Even though performance in the transition period can decrease in quality, it's also the time when the greatest creativity and growth can occur. As you've learned, that's what happened to Tiger. It's the price you have to pay to make the change. If done correctly, the price paid in the transition period is far less than the price paid if you stubbornly hang onto the first bar.

Stage Three—Embracing the New

In stage one, you release the old bar. In stage two, you fly through the air. In stage three, you grab hold of the new bar. The first stage of change of is an ending. The last stage of change is a new beginning, complete with the enhanced skills learned during the flight.

> *The only joy in the world is to begin.*
> —Cesare Pavese

In 1999 and 2005, Tiger embraced new and improved swings that took his game to a higher skill level. It's also important to remember that once you are on bar #2 for a matter of days, weeks or months, it becomes a bar #1, which means it will need to be released sometime in the future.

Three Improvement Methods

Just as there are three stages of change, there are three methods by which you can improve. Each of the methods has its place on the path to your dream.

1. Modeling

You learned about the power of modeling in the "Pre-Game Warm-Up" section of this book. You learned that to achieve any outcome in life, it's highly advantageous to find people who have already done it, and then pick their brains to discover their mental models and action strategies.

Tiger understands the power of modeling. In Tiger Trait #3, you read how he studied fifty great players and tried to combine the best of each of them to make himself even better. Do you take modeling as seriously as Tiger? I hope so. I'm also confident that you will use Tiger Woods as a superb model for success in your personal life and business.

2. Plussing

"Plussing" is a word Walt Disney coined for the process of continually making a series of small improvements. Walt loved to walk around Disneyland with his people and discuss how each attraction could be improved. He was constantly striving to "create a better show" for his guests.

Tiger makes plussing a vital part of his life as well. He is constantly making small improvements in his swing and his mental approach to the game. He knows that a series of small improvements in his golf skills will have the same effect as compound interest on a long-term savings account.

> *You should learn something from each*
> *and every round you play.*
> —Tiger Woods

3. Innovation

While plussing is a series of small improvements, innovation is one or more large improvements. Typically, innovations change the rules of the game and radically transform an industry or a life. Michael Dell transformed the computer manufacturing industry with his innovations in direct sales and just-in-time manufacturing. Steven Jobs is transforming the music industry with his iPod and iTunes innovations.

Tiger is an innovator in the world of golf. He has changed the rules of the game in three areas.

- **Team Tiger**—Golfers used to play the game with little help from others. The only exceptions were teachers who would occasionally advise them on their swings. Tiger puts together a constantly changing team of people who help him perform at his best. He has a business manager, a PR team, a swing coach, a caddy/body guard/ road buddy, a physical fitness trainer, a chef, as well as his wife and friends from his early years who travel with him and support him.

- **Physical Fitness and Nutrition**—Tiger has definitely raised the bar when it comes to physical fitness. With the help of a full-time trainer and chef, he has sculpted his body into one that looks and works like a professional basketball player. It wasn't always that way. A few years ago, golfers typically were overweight and out of shape. Tiger has changed all that. An increasing number of touring pros are buff like Tiger. They have to be, to keep up with Tiger's innovation.

- **Marketing and Public Relations**—With over $300 million in endorsement deals, Tiger is a marketing machine. He has taken marketing to levels attained only by his pal, Michael Jordan. In addition, his Tiger Woods Foundation is making a major difference in the lives of thousands of kids.

You Can Always Get Better

At the ages of ten months, ten years, twenty years, thirty years, and at every age in between, Tiger has been a fantastic golfer. He has maintained his skill level and dominance because he is always improving. His quote below sums it all up:

> "…it's a never-ending struggle, which is great. You can always get better! You can never get there. It's a journey with no arrival. And that's the beauty of it—that you can always become better the next day. It's pretty cool to think about it in that sense. Tomorrow I will be a better player than I was today."

Tiger Woods says, "Tomorrow I will be a better player than I was today." Can you say with Woods-ian conviction that you will be a better person tomorrow than you are today? Can you say that your business career and/or company will be better tomorrow than it is today? You can, if you make Tiger Trait #7 an integral part of your life.

Your Next Tiger Trait

Tiger has the athletic skills necessary to land $80 million in endorsement deals in 2006. But athletic skills aren't enough. There is another vital trait that must be in place to give the skills wings. You will learn about this trait, and how you can possess it, by turning the page and continuing down the path.

To discover Tiger Trait #10, go to
www.tigertraitsbookbonus.com now.

TIGER TRAIT#

BE LIKEABLE

AT ITS PEAK, the traditional TV golf audience is eight or nine Nielsen ratings points. Tiger's triumph at the 1997 Masters was the most watched golf tournament ever, with a rating of 15.8! This means almost half the audience was composed of nontraditional golf fans.

Tiger Woods is admired by millions of people of all ages, of diverse backgrounds, from all around the world. He is also well on his way to becoming sports' first billionaire. *ESPN Magazine* estimates that Tiger will earn $6 billion in his lifetime, 75 percent of which will come from product endorsements. In 2006, it's estimated that Tiger will earn $80 million in product endorsements from Nike, Buick, American Express, EA Sports, Upper Deck, Disney, Asahi Beverages, TLC Laser Eye Centers, TAG Heuer and others.

There are many reasons for Tiger's spectacular endorsement success.

1. **He is ethnically diverse.** Tiger has become a one-man symbol of globalization in the 21st century—a human United Nations. Early in his career he labeled his ethnic

heritage Cablinasian—a word that symbolizes a combination of Caucasian, Black, Native American and Asian cultures. Tiger doesn't want to be identified with just one culture. In response to a question about his ethnicity, Tiger issued this statement before a U.S. Open tournament: "The various media have portrayed me as an African American, sometimes Asian. In fact, I am both. The critical and fundamental point is that ethnic background . . . should not make a difference. Now, with your cooperation, I hope I can just be a golfer and a human being." Because of his ethnic commonality with billions of people worldwide, Tiger has a huge advantage in the marketplace because people tend to like people who are like themselves. It's a basic law of human nature.

2. **He's a winner.** People tend to connect and identify with winners because it makes them feel like winners too. At the end of the 2006 season, Tiger had won twelve major championships—two-thirds of the way to Jack Nicklaus' lifetime record of eighteen.

3. **He has a great story.** He is *Star Wars'* Luke Skywalker, *The Wizard of Oz's* Dorothy, and *Beverly Hills Cop's* Axel Foley rolled into one. As you learned in Tiger Trait #6, Tiger is on a hero's journey that is the basis of thousands of myths, stories, movies and books in all cultures. Tiger started from humble beginnings. He answered the call of greatness. He overcame internal and external resistances. He worked hard without any rewards at first. Finally, he rose to the top and won the internal prize of success and fulfillment and the external prize of financial riches. We all identify with people who are successfully completing the hero's journey.

4. **He has charisma.** As sports broadcaster Bob Costas said, "If you were from some other planet and were dropped into a professional golf tournament, you would be drawn to Tiger." His smile, his eloquence, his intelligence, and his presence all add up to a person you can't ignore.

5. **He is likeable.** Whether it's Tiger Woods, the Energizer Bunny, the Budweiser Frogs and Lizards, or George Foreman (who was third on the endorsement dollar list in 2002, behind Tiger and Michael Jordan), likeability sells. In a 1994 issue of the *Journal of Advertising Research*, David Walker and T. M. Dubitsky published an article entitled "Why Liking Matters," which was based on their extensive research. They concluded that if watchers like an advertisement and the people in it, they would "be more likely to pay attention to it and remember the message later." Studies also have shown that when people like someone, they will tend to believe that person.

Likeability: The Forgotten Success Factor

Tim Adams, the author of the wonderful book *The Likeability Factor* defines likeability as "the ability to create positive attitudes in other people through the delivery of emotional and physical benefits." I believe likeability is the overlooked secret to success. Think about it: There are hundreds of personal success books written each year. Most of them focus on the choices people must make in their daily lives to be successful. These books ignore one simple truth: Your success in life is determined primarily by other people's choices concerning you.

Isn't success in your personal life determined by who wants to be friends with you, who wants to spend time with you, and who wants to have a romantic relationship with you? In your business life, isn't your success determined by who wants to work with you, buy from you, be served by you, or be led by you? Think about the person who cuts your hair. Do you like him or her? Based on the thousands of people to whom I've asked that question, there is a 95 percent chance that you *do* like the person. Any business knows that, when the quality of the service and/or product is equal, likeability can mean the difference between one-time visitors and repeat customers.

If you're doubtful of the importance of likeability, consider the following.

- A 2002 study by the National Service Foundation revealed that likeable customers were three times more likely to have a positive service experience than unlikeable customers. People treated likeable customers better and gave them better service.

- In a study done in 1992 at the University of Toronto, Dr. Phillip Noll surveyed fifty divorced and fifty married couples. He found that likeable people had divorce rates 50 percent lower than the general population. If both partners were likeable, the divorce rate was reduced another 50 percent.

- The Gallup Organization has conducted a poll following every election since 1960. Of the three factors—issues, party affiliation and likeability—only likeability has been a consistent predictor of the winner.

- Dwight Eisenhower was elected president of the United States in 1952 and 1956 without any political or campaign experience. His opponent, Adlai Stevenson, had extensive experience in those two areas. What was one of the primary reasons Eisenhower overcame those two shortcomings? He was extremely likeable. He was a five-star general in World War II, and his troops loved him. He carried those positive emotions over into the election with his campaign slogan, "I Like Ike."

- Several studies have shown that likeable patients receive better medical care. A St. James University Hospital study, conducted in Leeds, England, showed that children with likeable parents received better health care, longer appointments, and more follow-up visits. A University of California study conducted by Barbara Gerbert revealed that likeable patients were encouraged to call their physicians and return for care more frequently.

Unlikeability Hurts

If likeable people get better service and have better relationships, then the opposite is also true: People tend to *not* hang around, do business with, follow, or support people they dislike. Consider the following:

- A study done in 1984 at the University of California showed that physicians gave less time to the patients they disliked and more time to the patients they liked.

- Alice Burkin, a leading medical malpractice lawyer says, "People just don't sue doctors they like." Research done by Wendy Levinson confirms Burkin's statement. As described in Blink: *The Power of Thinking Without Thinking* by Malcolm Gladwell, Levinson recorded hundreds of doctor-patient conversations. She then divided the doctors into two groups: those that had never been sued and those that had been sued at least twice. She found that the doctors who had never been sued (1) spent more than three minutes longer with their patients, (2) were more likely to engage in active listening by making statements such as, "Go on, tell me more about that," and (3) were far more likely to laugh or be funny during the visit. There was no difference in the amount or quality of the information they gave their patients concerning the patient's condition or details about medication. The difference between the doctors who were sued and those who weren't was entirely in *how* they talked to their patients, not *what* they said.

- The TV sitcom *Seinfeld* was hilarious to watch, but the four main characters were basically unlikeable. Jerry was a perfectionist and expected perfection from those around him. Elaine was materialistic and extremely picky. George was neurotic at best, and Kramer was just plain nuts. They had few friends outside of their foursome. None of them could maintain a romantic relationship or job for long. All were single and would remain so until they became... more likeable. The last episode was a true testament to their unlikeability. They were arrested and thrown in jail for not being helpful to a person in need. At the trial, all the people they had harmed through the years came back to testify against them. The *Seinfeld* characters were funny, but I don't think any of us would want them in our lives for long.

Likeability Helps in the Workplace

The hard stuff is easy. The soft stuff is hard.
And the soft stuff is a lot more important than the hard stuff.
    —Milliken & Company slogan

The "hard stuff" mentioned in the slogan above is buying the materials, making the product, and running the numbers. The soft stuff is managing all the relationships in a corporation. The soft stuff is always people-oriented, and likeability is a big part of working with and leading people. Consider the following:

- A Columbia University Study conducted by Melinda Tampkins found that success in the workplace is determined not by what you know or who you know, but by your popularity. Popular workers were seen as motivated, trustworthy, and hardworking, and received more promotions and pay raises.

- In *Fortune*'s "Best Companies to Work For" issue, Robert Levering wrote that organizations with positive employee relationships produce 15 to 25 percent more than average companies. This occurs because the managers have a strong connection with their employees, which creates loyalty. Such employees don't need to be micromanaged, and they will look for solutions to problems because they want to see their managers succeed.

- In the 1970s and 1980s, record-setting car salesperson Joe Gerard sold an average of five cars and trucks a day. He had two rules for success: (1) "Give my customers a fair price," and (2) "Be likeable." One way he showed his likeability was to send all of his 13,000 previous customers a holiday greeting card each month. The holiday greeting inside the card varied each month, but the face of the card was the same each month. It read, "I Like You." Joe knew that if you want people to like you, they must feel that you like them.

How to Become More Likeable

It is true that, for some, likeability seems to come naturally. Tiger Woods is naturally likeable, and through the years he has developed certain "people skills" that help him enhance his likeability. Even if you've never focused on likeability before, or you've had some challenges in this area, I believe that *everybody* can improve their likeability quotients. After all, Scrooge changed completely in one evening with the help of a few visitors. So can you—if you make likeability an important enough priority.

Answer the following questions. Be truthful; you also may want to receive some input from your friends and/or business colleagues who will give you honest feedback. Don't run away from the pain and difficulty caused by unlikeability. Just like Scrooge, you need to see the consequences of your past and present actions, and what these same actions will cost you in the future. In the same way, you need to get a clear picture of how much better your life will be should you focus on becoming more likeable.

- How has being unlikeable cost you in your personal life in the past? What is it costing you now? What will it continue to cost you in the future?

- How has being unlikeable cost you in your business life in the past? What is it costing you now? What will it continue to cost you in the future?

- How will being more likeable enhance your personal life in the future?

- How will being more likeable enhance your business life in the future?

Once you make a commitment to becoming more likeable, here are twelve ways you can do it.

1. Give compliments regularly.

Mark Twain said, "I can live for two months on a good compliment." The people around you agree with Mark, so compliment them regularly—preferably face to face. Compliment someone as soon as possible after a specific behavior. Begin the compliment with the person's name. Compliment a specific action. Explain why the action was important to you, and then tie a bow on the compliment by saying, "Keep up the great work!" When you give compliments, the other person wins. You do, too. You become more likeable, and you harness the power a primary rule of human behavior: Reward the kinds of actions you want to see more of.

> *Good thoughts not delivered mean squat.*
> —Dr. Ken Blanchard

2. Do little unexpected things for people.

The little unexpected things you do for people can have more power than the big expected things. Would women rather receive flowers from their guys on a special day such as Valentines Day, or would they rather receive flowers for no reason at all? Almost every woman I talk to says the latter. Why is this true? They're the same flowers. The reason is that flowers given for no reason at all are unexpected. The giver didn't "have" to buy them. Here's another example: Why do people play slot machines for hours? If they won a penny every time they pulled the lever or pushed the button, they wouldn't play long. That would be like having a job, and they already have one of those. They play because of the unexpected pay-offs.

3. Thank people.

On a regular basis, show the people around you how much you appreciate them. Mix it up. One time, thank them face-to-face. The next time, at the end of the day, write them a thank you note on a Post-it, so they see it the first thing the next morning. The next time, thank them when other people are around— this multiplies the appreciation effect. Then you might send a thank-you note to their home.

4. Make eye contact with others.

Have you ever met a person face to face, and you can tell they have been regularly ignored for years? You can see it on their faces, can't you? They either don't make eye contact with you or they sneak a quick peek at you and then look away. When you make eye contact with these people—or with anyone you meet—you acknowledge that they are important. It's a basic a human need.

5. Smile.

Tiger Woods has a terrific smile that he flashes often. So should you. Babies smile without being taught—sometimes as early as two days old. At its most basic level, a smile signals to others that you're a friend, not a foe. Look at the covers of the lifestyle magazines. Are the beautiful people gazing out at you usually frowning or smiling? Smiling, of course. That's a clue!

When you're smiling, the whole world smiles with you.
—Mark Fisher and Joe Goodwin

6. Use impactful words.

Some words have more positive impact than others, so try frequently to use words such as *absolutely, appreciate, awesome, enjoy, hello, love, magnificent, perfect, sure, welcome, wonderful* and *yes.* Use phrases and sentences such as "How can I help?" "It would be my pleasure," and "I'll personally take care of that."

> *Words are the voice of the heart.*
> —Confucius

7. Pay attention to the tone of your voice.

When it comes to communication, it's not only what you say but also how you say it. In fact, most communication studies show that how you say it is more important than what you say. Want to have an eye- and ear-opening experience? Audiotape or videotape your next presentation to a group or conversation with an individual. The tonality of your voice—and lack of it—will surprise you. Make sure your message is congruent by matching your tonality with your words.

8. Send "I" messages.

The best way to explain "I" messages is to contrast them with "you" messages. Here is a sample "you" message to a co-worker: "Bob, *you* did it again. *You've* done this over and over. *You* schedule us through lunch every day. We've talked about this several times, and *you* said you understood last time." "You" messages are often about blame. Here's the same conversation with an "I" message: "Bob, *I* have a concern. *I* noticed that we've been working through lunch a lot. *I'm* concerned the team might get burned out. Is there anything *I* can do to help you out with the scheduling again so this stops happening?" "I" messages create a dialogue rather than a blame session. They accomplish the result while maintaining connection with the other person. Often, the result is far better because the other person doesn't feel alienated.

9. Listen.

Pay attention both to people's words and the meaning behind the words. Listen until they stop talking. Take a second to formulate your response, and then talk. Interrupt only when you need to clarify something you heard.

> *Friendship consists of a willing ear,*
> *an understanding heart, and a helping hand.*
> —Frank Tyger

10. Share your feelings.

Ever wondered why Oprah Winfrey is such a popular and wealthy woman? In addition to her work ethic, drive, and intelligence, she is immensely likeable. A primary reason for this is she regularly shares her personal feelings and experiences with her audiences. She's not afraid to be human—the good, the bad and the ugly. You should share yourself, too. Carefully done, sharing your feelings will enhance your likeability and connection with those around you.

11. Learn to say "I don't know."

No one likes a know-it-all because everyone knows that no one knows it all. If you pretend to know everything, people will believe you about nothing. If, every once in a while, you say some form of, "I don't know," people will listen to you when you do know. The greatest talk show host of all time, Johnny Carson, had an endearing habit of saying, "I did not know that," when a guest made a statement that Johnny had never heard.

12. In business, show interest in people's personal lives.

At work, likeable people get hired more often and promoted more frequently. One way to be more likeable at work is to show an interest in people's personal lives. The "Marcus Welby Sandwich Technique" is a great way to do this. Marcus Welby was a family doctor on a TV show that ran for many years. He was absolutely great at connecting personally with his patients before and after he began his diagnosis. Here's his "Sandwich Technique": Whenever possible, every time you meet someone at work, talk about personal things for a few seconds. This is the top bread layer of the sandwich. As an example, "Jose, how's your son doing in soccer this year?" Then, get to the meat of the sandwich and talk about the business at hand. Just before you part ways with Jose, slap on the bottom layer of the sandwich by saying, "Say hi to Maria and Jorge for me."

Your Next Tiger Trait

Remember the Milliken & Company slogan cited earlier in this chapter: "The hard stuff is easy. The soft stuff is hard. And the soft stuff is a lot more important than the hard stuff." Likeability is a vital ingredient of the soft stuff. Two other key "soft stuff" ingredients are gratitude and giving back. At a relatively young age, Tiger Woods has added these two ingredients to his life and cooked up a winning recipe for the world. Read on to learn how to be grateful and give back.

TIGER TRAIT# ⑨

BE GRATEFUL, GIVE BACK

BACK IN TIGER TRAIT #3, "Select Teachers, Heroes, and Teammates Who Guide, Inspire, and Support," you learned about Tiger's stunning victory at the 1997 Masters. As Tiger teed off for his final round with a nine-stroke lead, Earl and Tida Woods were among the thousands lining the first tee and fairway. But another very significant man had made the trip from Pompano Beach, Florida, to witness Tiger's coronation. His name was Lee Elder. In 1975, Lee was the first African American to play in the Masters.

At the conclusion of the final round that wrapped up his twelve-stroke victory, Tiger walked off the eighteenth green to the historic Butler Cabin for a CBS interview and the fitting of the green jacket given to the Masters champion. Next up was the trophy presentation ceremony back on the eighteenth green. As Tiger left Butler Cabin, he spotted Lee Elder in the crowd and shouted, "Wait!" The assembled throng became strangely silent as Tiger motioned to the older man, saying, "Lee, come here." As the two men embraced—one, the first African American to play at the Masters, and the other, the first man of color to win the Masters—Tiger whispered in his ear, "Thanks for making this possible."

> *He who receives a benefit with gratitude*
> *repays the first installment on his debt.*
>   —Seneca

Tiger knows that gratitude is like a searchlight: It illuminates that which was always there. African-American professional golf pioneers Charlie Sifford (who played in the 1950s and 1960s but never received an invitation to the Masters) and Lee Elder were always there. Tiger cared enough to shine the searchlight of gratitude on them. Who has benefited from the illumination? Charlie Sifford and Lee Elder certainly have: They received the belated recognition they so richly deserved. But so did Tiger. He repaid the first installment on his debt to those who made it all possible. All of us who know this story benefit from it as well, because it reminds us to be grateful for all the gifts we enjoy.

Tiger has made an attitude of gratitude a way of life. Two years earlier, at the same course, Tiger repaid another installment on his debt. His win at the 1994 U.S. Amateur Championship gave Tiger an automatic invitation to play in his first Masters in 1995. Tiger played well enough in his first two rounds to make the cut. Then, at the end of the second day, young Mr. Woods did something that epitomized the person he had become. At six in the evening, after a long and emotionally draining day of golf, Tiger, still wearing his golf shoes, left the prestigious Augusta National Course and made a short trip to an overplayed municipal course. There, he met with the caddies of Augusta National. They were all African Americans.

Until 1982, all participants in the Masters Tournament were required to use the Augusta National caddies. Now, they were a forgotten group, as the professional golfers always brought their own caddies. Tiger wanted to express his gratitude to these men.

The act of expressing gratitude is valuable by itself, but it leads to another, even more valuable act—giving back—which is exactly what Tiger did after his visit with the caddies. On the same scruffy municipal course, he conducted a golf clinic for a group of young African American kids. Tiger had held golf clinics dozens of other times at tournaments around the country, but this time, with the Masters history as a backdrop, it had a special significance. Earl summed up the day when he said, "This is the culmination of a very hectic, long day. This young man has made his first cut in a PGA tournament, and he made it in a major championship. I've watched this young man pass from adolescence to manhood, and I'm very proud of him." From the beginning, his parents always said, "We've raised Tiger to be a better person than he is a golfer." That day in Augusta proved they had done their job well.

The Best Things in Life *Are* Free

In business, it's far too easy to get wrapped up in success and failure, gain and loss, profit and expense. We forget to appreciate what we have accomplished and the people who have helped us along the way. I believe that the true hallmark of success comes when we remember that the best things in life *are* free. Gratitude is a prime example of one of these best things. It costs you nothing to feel it, yet I believe gratitude is one of the least appreciated and experienced emotions in life. It is so powerful for three reasons.

1. **You win.** When you express gratitude, it reinforces how lucky you are to have empowering people and experiences in your life. The more gratitude you feel about the past, the happier you will feel in the present. You can't be grateful and unhappy at the same time.

   In addition, you will attract more in the future of what you express gratitude for in the present. Dr. Deepak Chopra said, "Where thought goes, energy flows." If you focus on what you don't have in life, you will end up with less of what you want. If you focus on what you do have, you will end up with more of what you want. The first step is to appreciate all that you have, and then you will be open to receiving more of what you desire. Using the time-honored "Is the glass half-full or half-empty?" question as a metaphor, be grateful for your half-full glass first, then life will fill the empty half. If you consistently express your displeasure for the missing half, life will drain your full half and you'll be left with an empty glass.

   > *My fiftieth year had come and gone,*
   > *I sat a solitary man,*
   > *In a crowded London shop,*
   > *An open book and empty cup*
   > *On the marble table-top.*
   > *While on the shop and street I gazed,*
   > *My body of a sudden blazed;*
   > *And twenty minutes more or less,*
   > *It seemed so great my happiness,*
   > *That I was blessed and could bless.*
   >
   > —William Butler Yeats

2. **They win.** When your gratitude is expressed to others, it reinforces their good deeds. They deserve to feel the recognition they have so richly earned. The key is that you must express your gratitude to them—preferably face to face. Your gratitude reinforces their positive behavior. Now, they're more likely to repeat it and gain more rewards. It's a never-ending cycle.

We make a living by what we get,
we make a life by what we give.
    —Winston Churchill

3. **Everyone wins.** When asked what was the most important question any human being needed to answer, Albert Einstein replied, "Is the universe friendly or not?" If you believe the world is not a friendly place, you withdraw from it and misguidedly have nothing to be grateful for. As a result, no one wins. If you believe the world is a friendly place, you engage the world at full speed, are grateful for its gifts and express your gratitude. As a result, everyone wins.

Gratitude is the memory of the heart;
therefore forget not to say often, "I have all I ever enjoyed."
    —Lydia Child

In a broader sense, I believe that gratitude is the moral memory of mankind. It reinforces the positive aspects of our cultures and perpetuates their existence. Gratitude feels good to the members of society and produces a cascade of beneficial social outcomes, because it reflects, motivates, and reinforces moral social actions in the receiver, the giver, and any onlookers. The fact that gratitude is universal across all cultures suggests that it is part of human nature.

In general, we in Western cultures don't like to think of ourselves as being indebted. We would rather view our good fortunes as the exclusive result of our own doing. As a result, we tend to neglect the practice of gratitude because it involves an admission of our vulnerability and dependence on other people.

I believe that the "them" or "me" dilemma can be solved with the power of "and." If you believe that your success is due to the gifts you've been given by other individuals in particular and society in general, and that you have taken the personal initiative to use those gifts well, then you can simultaneously be grateful to them *and* proud of yourself for all that you've accomplished in life. No one achieves anything by him- or herself alone. Coupled with his natural talent, Tiger Woods received the gifts of guidance, inspiration, and support from his teachers, heroes, and teammates. He had people like Lee Elder and Charlie Sifford who paved the way. Even the unknown individuals who cared for the golf courses, made his clubs, and lined the fairways to watch Tiger play have been part of his success. Now Tiger has become an "and" for thousands of young people throughout the world, by his inspiring example and by the work done by the Tiger Woods Foundation. He is providing opportunities for others to discover and develop their gifts, so they too may be proud of their accomplishments and share their good fortune with others around the planet.

Developing Your "Attitude of Gratitude" Habit

It's interesting to notice at what points in their lives people develop an attitude of gratitude. Some people need a near-death experience. Some people develop an attitude of gratitude only when something or someone has been taken. For example, a parent dies and the surviving family now feels more grateful for those who are left, or perhaps a man who has been unhappy about his spouse working all of a sudden loses his own job, and he feels blessed that his wife still has an income. Some people are grateful only once a year, on a Thursday in late November. But to gain the most from gratitude, don't wait for a near-death experience, the passing of a loved one or the third Thursday in November to be grateful. Do it every day. Make it a habit.

According to the dictionary, a habit is "a recurrent pattern of behavior that is acquired through frequent repetition." *Frequent* and *repetition* are the key words in this definition. It's vital that you internally and externally express your gratitude repeatedly throughout the day. This will keep you full of gratitude. The principle is similar to the common diet tip of pausing frequently while eating a meal to slow yourself down. This tip is effective because it takes the stomach about twenty minutes to register that it's full. Being grateful several times a day is like pausing while eating. It allows you to experience the "fullness" of your life on a regular basis in the present, and gives you the emotional energy to create more of the same.

Here's a four-step plan for creating your "Attitude of Gratitude" habit.

1. **Every morning:** While you're in the shower or on your way to work, count your blessings—literally. Answer this question, "What are ten people, places, things, and experiences I'm grateful for in my life today?" Don't do the same ten every day. Mix it up. Of the ten, create five new blessings every day. They don't have to be big blessings. Even small, usually unnoticed blessings are great. Here are some examples:

- I can breathe.
- The car started.
- My eyes work.
- The grass is growing.
- I spoke to a friend.
- The flowers look and smell great. (Stop and smell the flowers.)
- I have food to eat.
- The sun came up.
- My kids are doing fine.
- I have a job.

If you need to work hard to find blessings in your life, think of those who can't breathe because they're sick, or who don't have a car, or who are far away from friends and family. Imagine your life if these things or people were taken from you. If nothing else, acknowledge the gift of being able to think and feel in this moment.

There are two ways to live your life. One is as if nothing is a miracle. The other is as if everything is a miracle.

—Albert Einstein

2. **During the day:** On a regular basis during the day, express your gratitude to those who have helped or are helping you in life. It's the first installment on the debt you owe them. It can be almost anyone—family, friends, people at work, employers, employees, sales clerks, food servers, postal workers, the garbage collectors, or perfect strangers. Express your gratitude face to face, on the phone, by an email, or in writing.

3. **Right before you go to sleep:** Answer these two questions: (1) "What events or situations occurred today for which I'm grateful?" (2) "What people did I interact with today for whom I'm grateful?"

4. **Flip it:** Most people think worry is a completely negative emotion. This isn't true. Worry can be a signal to you that you need to "flip it." Worry always concerns the future. Gratitude is always experienced in the present. So, when you're worried about a negative event you don't want to have happen in the future, flip the thought to what you *do* have and then express your gratitude for it. Here are some examples:

   • Worried about losing loved ones? Flip it. Be grateful for them being in your life right now, and externally express your gratitude to them.

   • Worried about not having enough money tomorrow? Flip it. Be grateful for the possessions and money you currently have and your ability to earn more. Then take constructive action now to achieve your goals.

   • Worried about poor health in later years? Flip it. Be grateful for the health you have and your body's ability to regenerate, and take the appropriate actions right now to create better health.

*The invariable mark of wisdom
is to see the miraculous in the common.*
   —Ralph Waldo Emerson

Now that You're Grateful, Give Back.

The emotion of gratitude is important because people tend to feel obligated to give back. As you've learned, Tiger has the attitude of gratitude habit and gives back on a regular basis. The "share and care" philosophy was taught to him at an early age by his parents. In Tom Callahan's book, *In Search of Tiger,* Earl Woods remarked:

> If Tiger had wanted to be a plumber, I wouldn't have minded, as long as he was a hell of a plumber. The goal was for him to be a good person. He's a great person. He always had a gentle heart. There was a time when Tiger collected coins, gold coins. They were his pride and joy. One day, after seeing a TV documentary, he came to me with the coins and said, "Dad, could you send these to the kids in Africa?" Now I think everything he has given, and will give, is kind of like those coins.

Tiger gives many kinds of gifts to the world. For those of us who have followed his career, he gives us the gift of enjoyment and inspires us to strive for excellence as he does. Tiger's impact on children is tremendous. They love him, and he loves them. At one tournament, Tiger was swamped by hundreds of kids wanting his autograph. Tiger finally screamed, "Stop!" He pulled the smallest boy from the crowd, told the others to line up behind the boy and said, "No one gets an autograph unless you do."

Tiger wants to be a positive role model to children of all races and to provide for them educational experiences that prepare them for life. In Tiger's words, "The impact on kids is something I love to do. I love doing clinics. I love helping them out." In 1996, Tiger and his father established a non-profit foundation, the Tiger Woods Foundation*, so he could reach more kids and have a greater impact throughout the world. The theme of his Foundation is "Giving Love Back." As you've learned, *sharing* and *caring* are two key words in the Woods family.

The Tiger Woods Foundation mission statement is: "We empower young people to reach their highest potential by initiating and supporting community-based programs that promote the health, education and welfare of all America's children." Three of the projects of the Foundation are

1. **In the City Clinics.** In an effort to extend the reach of junior golf to the youth of the country, the Foundation began In the City golf clinic programs in 2003. Each three-day event features golf lessons on Thursday and Friday and a free community festival on Saturday.

    Tiger loves working with kids to help them achieve his dreams because he feels so many people have helped him along the way. He recognizes his responsibility as a role model for others. And he loves the smiles on the faces of the kids at his clinics—it helps him feel that he's touching the lives of children all over the world.

    In *Playing Through*, Earl Woods wrote, "Tiger tells the children, 'Look, there are no shortcuts in golf, and there are no shortcuts in life. You have to work for it. Dream big and keep your dreams to yourself. Because the dreams you have are those things that separate you

---

*A portion of the proceeds of this book is donated to the Tiger Woods Foundation. The author and this book are not endorsed by or affiliated with the Tiger Woods Foundation.

from others. If you give up your dream, you give up hope. And without hope, you are nothing.'"

2. **Start Something.** In 2000 the TWF and Target Corporation partnered to create "Start Something," a program that encourages children and teenagers to identify a specific personal desire or goal and begin taking steps toward achieving it. In the process, kids also develop the personal values, interests, and talents needed to attain their dreams. Program participants can qualify for scholarship awards that range from $500 to $5,000. Since the program's debut, Target Stores has awarded over $750,000 to scholarship winners, and more than two million children have been challenged to make their dreams a reality.

In many years of coaching, [Tiger] is the most focused in terms of important aspects of his life and goals. He is a giver, not a getter, and the product of two amazing parents.
—Wally Goodwin

3. **Tiger Woods Learning Center.** On February 10, 2006, the Tiger Woods Learning Center opened in Anaheim, California (a few miles from Walt Disney's dream, Disneyland). As described on the Tiger Woods Learning Center Web site, "The Tiger Woods Learning Center is here to get students thinking about the role education plays in their futures. We want to show them how to relate what they learn in school to their future careers. We offer exciting courses that revolve around careers in math, science, technology, and language arts. Because there is something for everyone at the TWLC, we hope to

show students how their personal interests can develop into an exciting career. And we do this all in a 35,000-square-foot facility, using the latest technology in a completely wireless environment.

At the opening, former President Bill Clinton told the crowd, "I'm impressed that Tiger Woods decided to do this when he was thirty instead of sixty." Tiger wrote, "My goal for the Tiger Woods Learning Center is to provide students with a place to explore their dreams and open doors to new opportunities and potential career paths. This is their center; and I hope it serves as a launching pad to great success. This is by far the greatest thing that has ever happened to me.

"This is bigger than golf. This is bigger than anything I've ever done on the golf course, because we will be able to shape lives."

The "You" Foundation

Imagine for a moment you had unlimited funds and unlimited time at your disposal, but only if (like Tiger) you put the time and funds toward creating a foundation that would bear your name. If you had a foundation like Tiger, what charitable projects would it be working on? It's usually best if your first projects involve those close to you—your family and friends. After that, you can move outward to your place of business and community. Then you can move outward even farther to your region, state, country, or world.

Most of us aren't yet at the point where we can create our own foundation. But fortunately, our giving doesn't have to be expansive in scope. A whole collection small "givings" done at the right times can be very beneficial. The actor Gary

Sinise went to Iraq in 2003 and discovered that thousands of children had no pencils or school supplies. When he toured an elementary school, he noticed four kids were sharing one notebook, three kids one pencil. So he created Operation Iraqi Children, asking people in the United States to bundle up pencils and other school supplies and send them to a warehouse in Kansas City. The packages were then shipped to an American base in Iraq, where the soldiers would distribute the supplies to schools throughout the area. Tens of thousands of children have the basic tools for learning, thanks to one man's caring and willingness to help, and the assistance of U.S. soldiers. A pencil can seem like a very small "giving," yet it can mean a better education for a child on the other side of the world.

In fall 2005, I saw a story on television about children from the Gulf Coast of Mississippi. Their homes had been destroyed by hurricane Katrina, yet these kids and their families gathered toys and small articles of clothing, packed them into cardboard shoeboxes, wrapped them, and shipped the boxes to children in Indonesia who had lost everything in the tsunami of December 26, 2004. These Mississippi children, who had lost so much, were excited and happy to do something for others. What they gave had very little monetary value, but the gifts meant so much emotionally for both the givers and the receivers.

What will your gift be? Where and how you choose to give may depend on what you're grateful for. Tiger is grateful for his early experiences with junior golf; hence the formation of his Foundation's In the City clinics. He is grateful for his dreams of golfing greatness that provided the fuel for his future success; hence the creation of his Foundation's Start Something program. He is grateful for the educational opportunities in his life; hence the genesis of the Tiger Woods Learning Center. So begin with what you're grateful for. That will point you to the where, what, and who of your giving.

You've now discovered and understood the most important secret of all success: gratitude for what you already have and appreciation for those who have helped you along the way. I believe that this trait is the one that Tiger will be the most proud of ultimately. As Winston Churchill implied, at the end of our lives we will gain far more satisfaction from what we have given to others than from any fame or fortune we may have acquired. Tiger's fame and fortune have allowed him to make an even bigger difference in the lives of others. Will you be able to say the same?

Congratulations! You've finished your round of "golf" with Tiger. I hope you've found your journey valuable and instructive. Now it's time to head for the clubhouse for your post-game cool-down.

YOUR POST-GAME COOL-DOWN

AFTER A GAME OF GOLF, most players go into the clubhouse to review their rounds and discuss how they did on the links that day—their triumphs and their tragedies. Let's do the same with the nine-hole round of Tiger Traits you just completed.

On hole #1, you learned how to identify and develop talents. You learned that you

- were born with a unique set of talents and weaknesses,
- should identify your unique talents and work on improving them, and
- should identify your weaknesses and work on managing them.

On hole #2, you learned that your talents are linked to your dreams, and that you need to create a clear and compelling dream that utilizes your talents.

On hole #3, you learned that you need to select teachers, heroes, and teammates who guide, inspire, and support you on the path to your dream.

On hole #4, you learned why it's so important to generate the confidence you need to bravely move down your path, and how your Long-Term Success Cycle of confidence, inspired action, and success will generate the positive emotions you need to handle the challenging portions of your journey.

On hole #5, you learned how, like Tiger, to manufacture four magnificent mental models that will produce empowering movies in your mind that will show you the way to your dream.

On hole #6, you learned how to let your actions do the talking. You discovered that you are on the hero's journey, like Luke Skywalker and Tiger Woods. You also learned how to enthusiastically and intelligently take action, and why it's so important to enjoy the journey.

On hole #7, you learned how to constantly improve with modeling, plussing, and innovation in both good times and bad while making your hero's journey.

On hole #8, you learned why being likeable is so important to a successful life. You discovered that people's decisions about you are just as important as the decisions you make. Finally, you learned twelve ways to become more likeable.

On hole #9, you learned why being grateful and giving back are two necessary ingredients of a fulfilled life. You discovered how to create an attitude of gratitude, and to whom you need to give back.

How did you do on your round? Which holes do you play well in your life, and which not so well? What are your best shots (i.e., a specific activity you do well within each Tiger Trait), and what shots do you tend to flub? Remember, like Tiger and all the greatest golfers, you really aren't playing against anyone but yourself. Tiger's goal is to get better with every round he plays. What's your goal?

In reality, *how* you did on this imaginary round of golf isn't as important as what you're going to do now. Remember that Tiger says you should learn something from every round of golf you play. What did you learn from the round you just completed, and what changes are you going to make in your life? After learning the nine Tiger Traits (modeling), the changes you make can be small (plussing) or large (innovation). What's important is to put the lessons of each trait into action.

All the beautiful sentiments in the world
weigh less than a single lovely action.
—James Russell Lowell

The Cycle of Life

There is a continuous cycle active in your life right now. This cycle is so powerful that it influences how you think and feel, what you do, what you have, and how much you are able to give to others. If you harness this cycle's power to your advantage, you will lead a rich life that will overflow with abundance. If you short-circuit this cycle, your life will never become what it was intended to be. I call this the *cycle of life.*

Cycles appear everywhere in nature: the seasons, day and night, acorns growing into oak trees and producing more acorns. Each cell in your body produces tiny bursts of energy by breaking down a sugar called glucose with the Krebs cycle. The earth replenishes its atmosphere by recycling its nitrogen in the nitrogen cycle.

Cycles are active in human behavior, too. Consider the Cold War between the United States and the Soviet Union. We built long-range missiles with devastating bombs that made the people of the Soviet Union feel threatened. So they built long-range missiles with devastating bombs to balance the power. That made the people of the United States feel threatened, so we built better long-range missiles with more powerful bombs. The cycle continued until both sides had enough missiles and bombs to blow everybody up a thousand times over.

Here's another example. A loving marriage is created by a man loving a woman and then expressing and demonstrating that love often. The woman feels loved and reciprocates. This makes the man feel loved and he reciprocates. And the cycle of love rolls on.

Back in Tiger Trait #4, you discovered that Tiger's unflappable confidence is created by the confidence cycle. Tiger feels confident. He takes inspired action. He achieves success creating enhanced confidence, which leads to more inspired action. When it comes to Tiger's confidence level, what goes around does come around.

All of the above cycles are self-sustaining. They occur naturally. Each ending leads to a new beginning. That's why they're so powerful and enduring. That's why you must understand and use the cycle of life.

Take a look at the diagram on page 141. It has four parts: *be, do, have,* and *give.* The four parts are connected as energy flows in a clockwise motion around the cycle. The cycle of life begins with *be.* Our language says it all. You're a human being, not a human "doing" or a human "having." It all begins with be.

> *If there is to be any peace,*
> *it will come through being, not having.*
> —Henry Miller

Your being encompasses all things internal—your spirit, character, natural talents, belief systems, mental models, and emotions. Tiger's internal being includes natural talent, mental toughness, and a caring spirit. What's yours? Why not create a To Be list before you create your To Do lists? When you create

The Cycle of Life

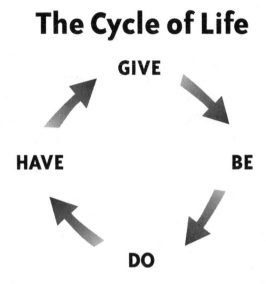

GIVE

HAVE   **BE**

DO

your compelling dream, include the person you want to be first. Then move on to what you want to do and the things you want to have.

Golf is what I do. It's definitely not who I am.
—Tiger Woods

The second part of the cycle of life is *do*. Doing includes all the actions you take in order to have things in your life. Being automatically leads to doing. Happy people do happy things. They smile. They talk about positive things in a cheerful voice. They don't have to make themselves smile; they smile because they're happy. The firefighters who stormed into the burning buildings on September 11, 2001, didn't have to psych themselves up or listen to motivational tapes. They did it because that's just who they were. Tiger naturally does things because of who he is inside. He wins golf tournaments because he is a fierce competitor. He gives back to people all over the world because he is a grateful and caring man.

The third part of the cycle of life is *have*. Doing automatically leads to having. You must take action in order to have knowledge, relationships, skills, positions, degrees, money, and material possessions. Tiger has tremendous golfing skill because he has practiced and trained for almost his entire life. Tiger has mountains of money in the bank because of his actions on the golf course and in the world of business.

The fourth part of the cycle of life is *give*. In order to give anything, you must have it in your possession. Teachers can give knowledge to their students because they have knowledge, have instructional skills and have teaching degrees. You can't give love to another person unless you have the love to give and have a relationship with the person. On the course, Tiger gives pleasure to millions of people around the world because he has awesome skills as a player. Tiger gives money and time to causes he believes in because he has earned the money and makes the time.

Take another look at the diagram on the previous page. Notice how the cycle of life becomes complete with the arrow pointing from *give* to *be*. Have you noticed that when you give to others, it enhances who you are? Now you can do more, have more, and give more, which further enhances your being ... and your cycle of life keeps rolling along.

> *One of the most fascinating things about golf is how it reflects the cycle of life. No matter what you shoot— the next day you have to go back to the first tee and begin all over again and make yourself into something.*
> —Peter Jacobsen

There is second way that your being can be enhanced. I believe that all our beings are connected to a universal power. All your life dreams are a small part of the universal dream. All the resources needed to achieve your dream are available to you from the universal power when you activate your cycle of life. You can connect with the universal power in many ways—prayer, meditation, or a walk in the woods, for instance. Tiger is unusual in that he was raised by parents who taught him Eastern and Western philosophies concerning the universal power.

> *I am—just as you are—a never-to-be-repeated event*
> *in this universe. Therefore, I have—just as you have—*
> *a unique, never-to-be-repeated role in this world.*
> —George Sheehan

The Cycle of Life

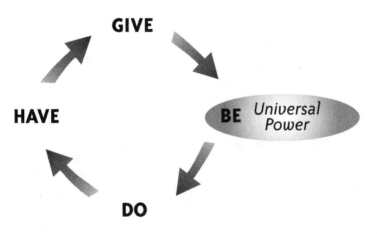

Here's where the cycle of life gets interesting. What happens to your being when you give to others? It's enhanced isn't it? That's why *give* continually leads to *be* in the diagram below. When you give, your being is now on a higher level than it was on the previous cycle. The cycle of life is now transformed into an upward spiral of life because a higher level of being leads to a higher level of doing, which leads to a higher level of having, which leads to a higher level of giving, which enhances the cycle even more. What goes around comes around. When you examine Tiger's life, you will see a vivid example of the upward spiral of life in action.

The Upward Spiral of Life

Here's a key concept in harnessing the power of the cycle of life. In order to change one part of your cycle of life, focus your attention on the other parts. As an example, have you ever tried to get up in the morning and be happy? Pretty tough to do, isn't it? Instead of trying to be happy, do happy things. Move like a happy person would. Smile. Have happy relationships. Have a job that makes you happy. Most important, give your happiness away. Look people in the eye and show them your smile. Compliment them. Tell humorous stories. Connect with the universal power in ways that bring you happiness. The bottom line is this: Don't try to be happy. Turn your attention on do, have, give, and connecting with

GIVE

HAVE

DO

BE

GIVE

HAVE

DO

BE

GIVE

HAVE

DO

BE

the universal power. Now the cycle of life will create happiness for you.

> *Happiness is like a butterfly.*
> *The more you chase it,*
> *The more it eludes you.*
> *But if you turn your attention to other things,*
> *It comes softly and sits on your shoulder.*
> —Anonymous

Here's another example of turning your attention to other things. If you want a new position in your company, quit trying to have the position. Focus on the person you need to be. What characteristics, attitudes and belief systems would this person possess? Focus on doing the behaviors that are necessary to gain the knowledge, skills and relationships that you will need. Focus on giving the kinds of support, service, and knowledge that make your company and the people in it better. Connect with the universal power to gain the insight and resources need. If you do the above, the cycle of life will automatically create the position you want to have.

Tiger Woods understands the cycle of life. From the stories in this book, I hope you see that, even though Tiger is attracting a cool $100 million a year, he doesn't focus on having money. He turns his attention to the other four components of the cycle of life—and the money magically appears.

There's a second benefit when you give to others. When they receive your gift, their cycles of life gain a jolt of positive energy and become upward spirals, too. Now both of your upward spirals of life are joined together. See the diagram on the next page.

The Connected
Upward Spirals of Life

Let's use the example of Tiger giving his time, enthusiasm, knowledge, skills, resources, and money to help create the Tiger Woods Learning Center. When children come to the Center, they learn to be better people. Their character, self-image, and belief systems are enhanced. They learn to do new and beneficial activities. By doing these activities they have improved skills, knowledge, relationships and resources. Now they can give more to others, which elevates their being —and their cycle of life spirals upwards. Tiger and all the TWLC kids are connected. They all benefit. And it all begins with Tiger's gift.

It's interesting to note that two connected upward spirals create what is called a double helix. Does the double helix diagrammed left look familiar? It should. Its form is the same as the DNA molecules in your body's cells. Your DNA is literally the stuff of life. Just as your parents DNA was given to create you. Your gifts to others will help create them. Be generous with your giving. The quality of your world and your life depends upon it.

In the interconnected universe, every improvement we make in our private world improves the world at large for everyone.
—Stephen Hawking

A Parting Shot

I love the following poetic comment Earl Woods (*Tiger: The Authorized DVD Collection*) once made about his son:

"Golf is not Tiger's primary mission in life.
He has a higher calling
    that will be manifested later in life.
I don't know what it will be.
But it will be humanitarian.
And it will be about children.
And it will be about caring and sharing.
He feels it, and I see it.
Now, we all have to wait and experience it."

I don't know about you, but I'm looking forward to experiencing it. I'm sure Tiger will follow his dad's advice, let his legend grow, and achieve his primary mission in life. When you integrate the nine Tiger Traits into your life and your business, I know you will do the same.

To discover Tiger Trait #10, go to
www.tigertraitsbookbonus.com now.

RECOMMENDED READING

Adams, Tim. *The Likeability Factor: How to Boost Your L-Factor and Achieve Your Life's Dreams.* New York: Crown Publishers, 2005.

Callahan, Tom. *In Search of Tiger: A Journey Through Golf with Tiger Woods.* New York: Crown Publishers, 2003.

Cialdini, Robert. *Influence: The Psychology of Persuasion.* New York: HarperCollins, 1998 (new edition).

Clifton, Donald and Paula Nelson. *Soar With Your Strengths.* New York: Dell Publishing, 1992.

Duran, Rudy with Rick Lipsey. *In Every Kid There Lurks a Tiger: Rudy Duran's 5-Step Program to Teach You and Your Child the Fundamentals of Golf.* New York: Hyperion, 2002.

Eammons, Robert A. and Michael E. McCullough, editors. *The Psychology of Gratitude.* New York: Oxford University Press, 2004.

Gerard, Joe with Stanley H. Brown. *How to Sell Anything to Anybody.* New York: Simon & Schuster, 1977.

Gladwell, Malcolm. *Blink: The Power of Thinking Without Thinking.* New York: Little, Brown, 2005.

Kanter, Rosabeth Moss. *Confidence: How Winning Streaks and Losing Streaks Begin and End.* New York: Crown Business, 2004.

Leonard, Tod. "Team Tiger," *The San Diego Union-Tribune,* 25 Jan. 2006, Buick Invitational section, 6.

Rosaforte, Tim. Raising the Bar: *The Championship Years of Tiger Woods.* Collingwood, PA: Diane Publishing Co., 2002.

Sinise, Gary. "How Do You Spell Relief?" *O, The Oprah Magazine*, Oct. 2004.

Thomas, Bob. *Walt Disney: An American Original.* Disney Editions, 1994.

Tiger: The Authorized DVD Collection. Burbank, CA: Buena Vista Home Entertainment, 2004.

Vogler, Christopher. *The Writer's Journey: Mythic Structure for Storytellers and Screenwriters.* Studio City, CA: Michael Wiese Film Productions, 1992.

Wind, Jerry and Colin Crook with Robert Gunther. *The Power of Impossible Thinking: Transform the Business of Your Life and the Life of Your Business.* Upper Saddle River, NJ: Wharton School Publishing, 2005.

Woods, Earl with Fred Mitchell. *Playing Through: Straight Talk on Hard Work, Big Dreams and Adventures with Tiger.* New York: HarperCollins, 1998.

Woods, Earl with Pete McDaniel. *Training a Tiger: A Father's Guide to Raising a Winner in Both Golf and Life.* New York: Harper Collins, 1997.

Woods, Tiger with the editors of *Golf Digest. How I Play Golf.* New York: Warner Books, 2001.

ABOUT THE AUTHOR

FOR OVER TWENTY-FIVE YEARS Nate Booth has been studying, applying and assisting others in the art of thriving in times of rapid change. Nate received his DDS degree from the University of Nebraska in 1971 and a master's degree from the same school in 1983. From 1987 through 1997, he worked closely with Anthony Robbins in the creation and presentation of corporate training programs.

In addition to *Tiger Traits,* Dr. Booth is the author of the books *Thriving on Change: The Art of Using Change to Your Advantage* and *The Diamond Touch: How to Get What You Want by Giving Others What They Uniquely Desire.* All three books contain compelling personal and business success strategies for a world playing a game with a new set of rules.

Dr. Booth creates customized presentations and training programs for corporations and associations world-wide. His clients include Aetna, Century 21, Dow Chemical, IBM, Inc. Magazine, Kraft Foods, Mobil Oil, NASA, National Automobile Dealers Association, Northwestern Mutual Life, Oracle, Principle Financial Group, Saturn Corporation, Siemens and Wells Fargo.

For more information, call 800-917-0008 or visit www.natebooth.com.

INDEX